To Nell
with all
friendship
Alan

The Little Yellow Train
Survival and Escape from Nazi France
(June 1940 - March 1944)

ALAIN F. CORCOS

ℭℴ

TOWN HOUSE PRESS
Pittsboro, North Carolina

Library of Congress Catalog Card Number 96-60039
International Standard Book Number: 0-940653-42-7

Printed in the United States of America

Original maps by Maria C. Weber
Lakewood, Ohio

৪০

The author dedicates this book
to his brother, Gilles,
who is so much part of it.

Acknowledgments

This book could not have been written without the encouragement and kind criticisms of Floyd Monaghan, Susan and Sharon Rutten, Wayne and Nancy Claflin, Evelyn Rivera, Ralph Lewis, Lois Zimring, Henry Silverman, Michael and Steve Hack. Special thanks to Sara Wosko for her outstanding editorial assistance and Marguerite Rousset who permitted the author to record and draw on her account of the liberation of the Briançonnais, that part of France that the he learned to love so long ago. Finally, he wants to express his gratitude to his wife, Joanne, for passing long hours copyproofing the manuscript.

Contents

Part 7. The Escape

Part 8. Join the French Air Force and See The United States

Epilogue, 201

Part 9. The Liberation of the Briançonnais

A Personal Note to the Reader

This is the true story of my brother and myself living in Southern France during World War II, first under the Vichy Government and then under the Italian-German occupation. In March of 1944, we escaped from France through Spain, joining up with the Allied Forces in North Africa while still in our teens. I decided to tell our story after taking a sentimental journey back to our homeland forty years later retracing the steps of our dangerous escape from the Alps to the Pyrenees.

This book has been written with primarily an American readership in mind who for the most part have never experienced events I describe. It is more than a recounting of our escape from France, and more than an account of two French brothers living through these horrible war years, for I have tried to reveal what I thought and felt at the time, so far as I can recall, and how I feel now more than forty eight years later. While writing this book I finally had to ask myself in what ways my experiences throughout World War II fashioned my world views and governed my actions. I wondered how my life would have been different; what would have been my inner feelings and thoughts had I not gone through these experiences.

As with everyone, some of my behavior has certainly been affected by my teen age experiences. For example, there was so little to waste during wartime that I have always found it difficult to throw anything away, and because I was so hungry during four years of my life, I have never wasted any food since. I have never cared for fancy automobiles, a car being only a means of locomotion. As long as it has an engine and four wheels and works when needed I am happy. Only recently, now that I am older, have I looked for comfort in a car. This lack of appreciation for automobiles can be understood when one realizes that when I was growing up in France during the war years, there were no cars to drive and the only means of personal locomotion faster than walking was bicycling. I hate to queue up even for five minutes because it reminds me too much of the long lines that my mother had to stand in during the occupation in order to feed her family.

My philosophical outlook on life has also been affected; in some ways positively and in others negatively. Because as a teenager I had to cope with and escaped death at the hands of French and German Nazis, as an adult I put up with lots of things that others who have not had my experience will not put up with or have a terrible time coping with. As a result I have found myself able to ride out life storms more easily than many of my friends. For example, I never considered that the loss of a job was the end of the world; for I always found a better one. As another example, having lived under a dictatorship, I know the value of freedom of expression and never miss the opportunity to vote, even when I believe that my vote will not make much difference.

The unfortunate consequences of my experience as a teenager include an inner cringe every time I hear the German language, even though I am aware that new generations are different from old ones. I am still reminded of the German troops goosestepping through the French streets singing patriotic songs and of the German warnings given through loudspeakers in railway stations. As a scientist, I have had a few opportunities to visit Germany, but every time I went there, I felt very uncomfortable. When my own children became teenagers, I had a terrible time understanding them and had to rely on my wife to teach me to be an understanding father. She helped me understand that I had been robbed of my own teen age life and forced to mature too quickly.

In some ways, however, I do not believe my life would have been different at all if my teen years had been less traumatic. For instance, I doubt very much that my experiences during the war had any bearing on my professional life. If someone had asked me as a child what I wanted to be when I grew up I could not have given him or her an answer. However, people around me knew that I loved to grow plants and that in some way I would always be connected with them. They were right. At first I was a horticulturist, then a plant breeder, and finally ended up my professional career as a University Professor of Botany. I grew carnations on the French Riviera and peaches in California. I carried on genetic researches with a very small plant akin to watercress in test tubes in air conditioned growth chambers. Growing plants has always remained in my blood, or should I say in my genes, since I am a geneticist. In this respect I have never changed.

I also doubt I would have been any less of a fighter against racism if I had not been discriminated against in my youth for not belonging to the master race.

For years friends encouraged me to write the story of my escape from France. In 1984 I started to think about it seriously, but the first version of the book dealing solely with my escape was heavily criticized. It seemed that the readers did not really understand why it became necessary for my brother and I to escape from France. The questions early readers of the book raised indicated that I must give more insight into the conditions in the France of that period and that I should attempt to describe the feelings of my parents, my brother and myself during this time. Recapturing our feelings was very difficult to do for two reasons. Firstly, no diary was ever kept by any of us, and though I have a good memory, the thoughts and feelings that are expressed in the book are as I remember them forty- eight years later. I have tried to make a distinction between my thoughts as a teenager and those of the older man. Secondly, until I started to write this account I had always tried to forget this awful period of my life when I was often hungry and persecuted for having ancestors whose religious beliefs I did not share. I had not only to remember it, but paint it in detail.

Despite these difficulties I finally decided to go ahead with the book just after the Gulf war. To me Saddam Hussein is another Adolf Hitler. Like Hitler, Hussein is a warmonger who practices genocide. His victims are Kurds instead of Jews. Unfortunately, we are not rid of Hussein as we are of Hitler, nor is Saddam Hussein alone in getting away with this behavior. Throughout the world people are still exterminated for no other reason than they belong to some different ethnic group causing one to wonder if there has been any moral progress in the world.

While writing this book, I continually asked myself, particularly in the beginning why I should write about my experiences if they were only my own. But they were also the experiences shared by many young men and women in France at the time. It is these young people who became the French of the 50s, the 60s and 70s. Whatever they were, the war left a mark on them for the rest of their lives. Also, while writing this book, I became convinced that it should be not only about my escape from Nazi France, but also a personal account of my recollections of a period of a brutal dictatorship, repression, persecution and betrayal and of a period of courage, devotion, friendship and love.

A.F.C.
East Lansing, 1992

PART 1

THE WAR

September 1939 - June 1940

CHAPTER 1

The War Breaks Out

The time has come when the last illusions of the British Government had been dispelled. The Cabinet was at last convinced that Nazi Germany meant war....
WINSTON CHURCHILL (1939)

March 1939 found my brother Gilles and me, 12 and 13 years old respectively, in England. Our parents had brought us to London so that we might gain a command of the English language, for they rightly believed that English rather than French, was to become the international language. They situated us with a dentist and his wife who took in boarders for extra income. The family we boarded with, whose name I do not recall, did not speak a word of French. This was conducive to our parents'desire, but their intentions were largely thwarted by the fact that all through the day Gilles and I spoke our native tongue while attending the French Lycée in London, where we needed to complete the school year we had begun in France. A foreign language, of course, is best mastered when one does not speak one's native language for months at a time. Hence, it would have been more productive if my brother and I had attended separate English schools.

This oversight on the part of our parents may have been due to the anti cipation they felt toward celebrating their twenty-five years of marriage by touring Canada and the United States while Gilles and I were in England. Yet I should explain, lest the reader conclude that we were left in the hands of complete strangers, that on weekends, Gilles and I frequently stayed with a family living in Ingleside, a suburb of London, whom our parents had known for many years. Mrs. Evans was French and had first met my father in Paris before World War I. It is possible that there might have been some romance between the two, but I have never been sure. Mr.Evans, her husband, was a well-to-do English business man. They had two sons, older than Gilles and I were. One was called Jean Paul and the other had my name, Alain François. I doubt that this was a coincidence. Our weekends with the Evans were thoroughly enjoy-

able since we could play tennis and watch television, a new form of enter-
tainment. I still remember the small and not very powerful sets of the
time, but what a change from the radio. After all, now we could see who
was talking.

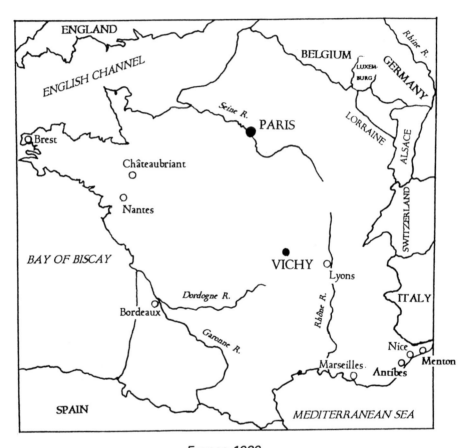

France 1939

After finishing our school year in London, Gilles and I attended a
small private school in Yorkshire during July to further improve our
English. After two weeks, however, we were miserable. The food was
atrocious and the teachers were not at all interested in our progress. We
wrote to Mrs. Evans explaining how we felt and she in turn sent a

telegram to our parents in the U.S. Father then telegramed the principal of the school requesting that we be returned to London, citing the possible outbreak of war in Europe as the reason for his request rather than the conditions of the school. This was apparently accepted as a valid reason for our leaving the school as many people at this time had grown increasingly convinced that war in Europe was inevitable. Only a year earlier England and France had attempted to appease Hitler by giving in to his territorial demands in order to maintain peace. But it was evident that Hitler was not contented with having swallowed up Czechoslovakia and Austria for his sight was now on the capture of Poland. By 1939, appeasement had given way to a determination that Germany should expand no further. War would become inevitable if Poland was invaded. Thus it was decided that Gilles and I would spend the rest of the summer with Mr. and Mrs. Evans until our parents could return for us. On our way back to London by train, however, we found ourselves in a serious predicament—at least for teen aged boys—, for after purchasing our tickets we were left with very little money for lunch. It became immediately apparent that we could not afford the regular lunches presented on the menu, but after some discussion we finally solved the crisis by resolving to be content with two sardine sandwiches. This allowed us to arrive in London with half a pound in our pockets.

We then passed the whole month of August with the Evans, playing tennis and swimming in their pool until our parents, increasingly worried about the situation in Europe, finally arrived. Unknown to Gilles and me at the time, our parents had already discussed a temporary move to the United States. Father had fought in W.W.I and understood in a way we did not, and could not, the tremendous horrors of war. At fifty-five years of age, he was well aware that he would not be called upon to serve and also that there was little chance that Gilles and I would reach the age when we would be summoned. Father was anxious, though, that his family should not witness, or in any way be a part of another war. The dispersement of families or entire populations, the death of thousands of young men, and the suffering and anxiety inflicted on those who served at the battlefront as well as on their loved ones were experiences he wished to shield us from. He had suffered the effects of mustard gas during the first world war after which he spent many months recovering with the help of our mother who nursed him back to health. But the psychological effects of fighting in the trenches were so devastating that many soldiers, including Father, could not bring themselves to speak of their experiences for many years afterward. When Father finally did begin to relate his war experiences, our pacifistic beliefs were reinforced and a contempt for politicians and generals who sought to glorify themselves through battles of attrition grew within us.

Father realized, as must have many others who served in World War I, that France had lost a million men in a war that had no reason to be fought. The assassination of one man, the Austrian Archiduke, Francis Ferdinand, at Sarajevo by a Serb, led to the death of millions because it gave Austria an excuse to gobble up Serbia in its attempt to expand eastward. Because of diplomatic ties between Austria and Germany on the one hand, and Serbia and Russia, Russia and France, France and England on the other, Europe was aflame for four years. The death of one man and the ambitions of European national leaders condemned the young men of their nations to die or suffer serious, often debilitating wounds, while existing under absolutely atrocious conditions of stench, filth and continuous fear. Sleep was constantly interrupted in the trenches at the battlefronts. Food and even water was lacking. Thousands of young men, no matter what their prior calling had been, were informed that their only duty now was to kill as many as they could of the other young men who lay in the trenches across from them in order to keep the enemy from advancing. Father told us of a few unwritten rules established between the German and the French soldiers—out of a sense of common humanity no doubt— one of them being no shooting if the man across the trench had his pants down.

In contrast to the soldiers who actually fought the battles, the high brass, the generals with their staff, lived in the comfort of requisitioned houses located miles behind the battle lines, eating excellent meals and discussing how they could win a few skirmishes so that their names would appear in the national news. This of course would lead to a promotion sooner or later. Father told us what seemed to us to be a fantastic, but true story indicating how little the high brass concerned themselves over the deaths of a "few" soldiers as well as how easily generals could be fooled by their own troops. According to our father, his brigade received orders to make an attack, but no one in the brigade wanted to do any more fighting that particular week, including the captain and the two lieutenants, so they conjured a plan that allowed them to seemingly follow orders without actually carrying out the attack.

Since it was well known that the officer who gave the order never came into the trenches, the captain of the brigade drew up a fake battle plan and withheld the names of the soldiers who had been killed or wounded the day before the alleged skirmish was to take place. A sergeant who was prone to tattle was given a sudden permission to see his wife. The day of the "battle" came and went with nothing actually happening, but the following morning an official report appeared stating that valiant soldiers had pierced the front along a mile and half the previous day. They had advanced two miles beyond the trenches, taking a few prisoners, but under extremely heavy fire, had been repulsed and the prisoners had escaped. The losses were light; a few soldiers killed, a few wounded. At headquarters the officer in charge was pleased, while the soldiers under him had a quiet day.

Another of Father's stories illustrated how different were the views generals and fighting men held toward the war. One general, who will remain nameless, returned from horse-back riding one day to see the house in which he temporarily resided completely destroyed by a bomb dropped by a Zeppelin. Realizing that had he been in the house he most likely would have perished, he felt that the Germans had over stepped the rules of fair play during warfare. It was permissible to kill soldiers on the front, but quite another thing to endanger generals a good distance away. So this general, being quite incensed with this act, had himself driven 100 miles to the chief of staff's headquarters in order to complain about the behavior of the enemy. His superior, General Joffre, responded: "What do you want me to do, declare war on the Germans?"

Father's position as an anti-militarist became increasingly understandable to me after hearing stories such as these, and I came to share his opinion that it was the soldiers in the trenches, not those in command, who had won the battle of Verdun, the turning point of the war. For it was they, the foot soldiers, who endured hell for two weeks —shooting at everything that moved across from them, losing their friends and fellow soldiers by the thousands, eating rats, drinking dirty water, living in undescribable scum and filth, totally isolated from other units as well as from the high command who had no idea what was going on. Father and his friends found themselves without any water, except some rain water that had percolated into a shell hole. After having drunk all of it, they found a corpse at the bottom of it. In spite of having boiled the water on a small alcohol lamp that Mother had sent him, Father became very sick and suffered for years from inflamation of the kidneys.

Now, twenty-three years later, Father realized that so far two generations of Corcos' had gone to war against the Germans—his own father in 1870, he and his brothers in 1914. Would there be a third generation? He declared to himself, if not to us, "that enough was enough," and he thought he could best protect his family from the ordeals he had endured by moving us to the United States.

Beyond his own war experience, an equally compelling reason for Father wanting to get us out of Europe could have been the rising anti-Semitic fervor not only in Germany but in many parts of Europe including France. While neither my parents nor Gilles and I were practicing members of the Jewish faith or any other faith, we did have ancestors who were, a fact that made us Jews in the eyes of antisemites. Our father did not need a crystal ball to guess that, if Hitler were victorious, our future would be bleak. What Hitler would do was explicitly stated in his book, *Mein Kampf*. He would eliminate all his enemies, in particular the Jews whom he considered vermin, "akin to the cholera bacillus." Hitler was a firm believer in the natural inequality among groups of peoples. He believed in the existence of separate and distinct races and that the desirable qualities are found in some "races", but not in others. According to him—and some German and French pseudo-scientists before him—, the best race happened to be the "Aryan" race, the bearer of human cultural developement that was destined to rule the world. The very existence of world civilization depended upon maintaining and safeguarding the purity of the Aryan race which was carefully defined so as to include the Germans and their friends, such as the Japanese who became the Allies of Hitler in 1941. According to Hitler the most despicable race happened to be the Jews who were responsible for all the evils that plagued humanity in general and Germans in particular. By 1938, it was obvious to anyone who was paying attention to what was going on in Germany and Austria that Hitler had already started his murderous program concerning the Jews in these two countries.

It would have been easy for our father to move us out of Europe. After the First World War he had been very successful in the glass industry. In

1932, he sold his company and retired early in order to enjoy other pursuits. He had invested part of his money in a flower farm on the French Riviera where we lived and the rest in stocks and bonds. Consequently, all that he had to do was to have his money wired to a U.S. bank and send Gilles and I two tickets for passage to New York where we would have known the pleasures of American teenagers. The only obstacle to his plan lay in the fact that our mother who was very close to her own mother and sisters expressed her wish to return to France and this was what our parents did. Later, Mother admitted that it had been a very poor decision on her part.

So, our parents arrived in London on August 28 and the four of us flew from London to Paris on August 31 where we spent a few days with our maternal grandmother. The war broke out September 3. Immediately we experienced our first air raid alerts. Untroubled, in the basement shelter, I played chess with my cousin, Francis, until it was safe for us to come back up. Francis was six months younger than me and two years later he was to share our lives. Shortly afterwards we left for the French Riviera where our home lay since 1932, just outside the town of Menton at the French-Italian border.

In order for the reader to understand and appreciate what happened to our family during the war years the next three chapters deal with the history of France from September 1939 up to March 1944 when Gilles and I escaped from France. Many history books have been written on this sad period. Though all the authors of these books do agree on the important events that occured then, they do not judge with the same severity the Vichy government that ruled France from June 1940 to June 1944. In general, the historians of the 1950's were lenient. Those after 1971 were not. The former tried to defend the Vichy Government which collaborated with the Nazis by stating that without such a collaboration French people would have been worse off. The latter condemned Vichy as a fascist, reactionary, and vicious government. The historians have been handicapped because most of the official documents having to do with that period are under lock and key and will not be available to them before 2004 A.D.

I have always believed that the Vichy Government was indeed a fascist government, similar to the one of Hitler. I was sure of it when I was a teenager living under it and I have not changed my opinion after having read more about that period.

CHAPTER 2

The Phoney War, The Real War And The Armistice: September 1939-June 1940

Airplanes are interesting toys, but they have no military value.
MARSHALL FERDINAND FOCH (1911)

Now, as I see it, the enemy will not attack us for a considerable time. It is in his interest to let our mobilized and passive army "stew in its own juice", while at the same time he is busy elsewhere. Then when he thinks that we are weary, confused and dissatisfied with our inertia, he will finally take the offensive against us possessing completely different cards in the psychological and material line from those he holds at present.
COLONEL CHARLES DE GAULLE (OCTOBER 1939)

During the first eight months of World War II neither France nor England was actively engaged in the land war. Though both countries had agreed to launch a series of attacks on Germany to help Poland defend herself against the onslaught of the Wermacht, the engagements were merely skirmishes and did not in any way prevent the Polish forces from capitulating. The Germans moved with such striking rapidity and such force that the war in Poland was over before England and France could come to grips with the military situation confronting them. For eight months—until May 1940—the war on the Western front would be a "phoney war" or as the French said, "drole de guerre" where really nothing would happen. The French Army had planned for a defensive war with massive fortifications, the Maginot Line, and not for an offensive war, possibly because they did not have the right equipment, training, or worse the state of mind. And so, apart from the initial skirmishes, most of the soldiers never fired a shot throughout the fall and the winter months. A kind of torpor pervaded the English and French troops who became very discouraged. After all, they had been dragged from their homes to find themselves in a mock war, being bored to death. If France and England had fallen into a somnolence, Germany continued to rearm, overhaul equipment and train more men, in order to crush the Allied forces in due time.

However, the war was real in other places in Europe. The Soviet Union that had only recently become the ally of Germany invaded Finland. This small country, to the astonishment of the world, managed to fight the Red Army for a while, but in the end had to capitulate. Norway also became a battleground, when England and France felt obliged to prevent the deliveries of Swedish iron ore through Norway. During the winter months, the Swedish ports were icebound and the ore had to travel by rail to the Norwegian port of Narvik and thence by ship to Germany. To stop the traffic the Allies could have mined the inland waterways between Dennmark and Norway. This would have forced the Norwegian ships to sail on open seas and be attacked by the Royal Navy. But before the Allies made up their mind to do this, the Germans invaded Dennmark and Norway.

War at sea also was far from phoney. It was to be a life and death struggle waged by England to preserve her lifelines, her sea-communications with her empire and other nations. Since England had to import much of the foodstuffs and raw materials that she needed, she had to prevent Germany from strangling her by driving her commerce off the seas. The battle of the Atlantic began immediately in 1939 and continued throughout the entire war, reaching its peak in 1942.

In the Spring of 1940 all hell broke loose. The German forces overran Holland in five days, subdued Belgium in eighteen days, conquered France in six weeks. The German victory over these three countries is one of the most dramatic military campaigns on record. It was the first demonstration of what the Germans called the blitzkrieg, literally the lightning war. But this idea of fighting was not original with the Germans. In fact during the 1930s a French officer named Charles de Gaulle had written a book called *Vers l'Armée de Métier*, The Army of the Future, in which he suggested that in order to win a modern war it would be absolutely necessary to use a highly mobile striking force centered around tanks, self-propelled guns, and trucks to transport the infantry. Such a force would rapidly penetrate into enemy territory, break front lines, wreck command areas and cut rear supply routes. Completely disorganized, the enemy would be unable to coordinate a defense against the infantry that would follow the striking force.

Unfortunately for France, the French High Command did not agree with the vision of de Gaulle and though France had quite a few tanks, it continued to deploy them in an antique fashion throughout the Army instead of concentrating them into powerful motored divisions. On the other hand, the German High Command took de Gaulle's advice and created "panzer" divisions that permitted the German forces to blitzkrieg in the Spring of 1940. They invaded Belgium and Holland May 10; they reached the Ardennes May 13, occupying Sedan the same day; they cut a swath across Northeastern France from the Belgian border to Abbevile on the coast. The last French attacks against the Germans were made by Colonel de Gaulle who finally had an armored division at his disposal. But unfortunately these attacks scarcely hindered the German advance. So were the efforts of another officer who, like de Gaulle, would play a role in the future of France. This man was General Giraud who was sent to reorganize and reassemble the French troops when the Ardennes sector collapsed. He failed completely and was taken prisoner May 18.

Blitzkrieging again the Germans surged westward, reaching the sea around Dunkirk on May 20th; they stopped there for reasons which are still unknown. This permitted the English forces and part of the French forces to be miraculously evacuated. The Germans reopened the battle on June 5, reached the Seine River on June 8, and crossed it on June 10. The French defenses having crumbled, the Germans raced towards Paris which fell in their hands June 14. In front of them many civilians and much of the French military personnel were retreating in complete disorder.

This exodus had started small, but then it grew very fast to reach an incredible size. First, there were only the refugees from Holland and Belgium, then those of Northern France. But after June 5, when the allied front crumbled, hundred of thousands of French people were on the road going South. Such an immense exodus was exploited or even masterminded by the German High Command, for it knew that this procession of a large number of people on the roads would prevent reinforcements of the Allied Armies reaching the battlefronts. To gain this objective the Germans made sure that someone in every village (it was either a German or a German sympathizer, a member of what had been called the Fifth Column) who, as soon as the first bombs fell, would tell the inhabitants, "Go immediately away from here, for the village is going to be destroyed. The army will follow, then the Gestapo. And you know how the Poles were treated by the Gestapo." Panic was the order of the day. Nothing is more contagious than flight. Whole villages left, including the priest, the mayor and the civil servants. People left their homes with as many of their possessions as they could loading them onto their bicycles carts, trucks, and buses. It was an extraordinary sight: a paralyzing tangle of refugees and retreating French troops. Everyone was on the road not knowing where to go; rich people being driven by their chauffeurs; middle class people driving their own cars; peasants driving their horse carts; cyclists and pedestrians slowly moving on the edges of the roads. It was a migration of fear, panic, despair, uncertainty, hardship and a sense of injustice. Amid the chaos of this mass exodus thousands of young children became separated from their parents. Some would be reunited with them. Some would not.

To increase the panic, German airplanes were shooting at the stalled fugitive processions. Constantly exposed to gunfire on the tree-lined roads, cross roads, bridges, closed railroad crossings, many of the refugees regretted that they had fled from their homes. Though they had found it dreadful to sit there, doing nothing, waiting for bombs to drop and for the Germans to arrive, they soon discovered that to be on the road was ten times worse. Everything in this flight was ghastly. To be fired on, to attempt, often in vain to get food, water and gasoline at black market prices, was too much.

France without Paris was now like a body without a brain. It seemed to have been abandoned by its government and by its army. A few days before the fall of Paris the French government had retreated south of the Loire, then moved to Bordeaux. French people were still hoping that the Germans would stop somewhere. They could not admit that there was not a battlefront anymore. They thought that the Generals had a plan. If the army could not hold Paris, it would certainly defend the Loire River line. It was impossible for France to simply collapse. But the truth was otherwise. France was indeed collapsing, and on the road the exodus became an uninterrupted flow of cars, trucks, oxcarts, bicycles all loaded with all the possessions that their owners had been able to load onto them then they left their homes. People were soon exhausted and having lost control of their lives, were crying out for help, but there was no one to help them for the French administration had broken down completely. They were left to their own devices on the long dusty roads hungry, thirsty, desperate, and panic-striken as they were fired upon by the German fighter planes. Some were killed by the wayside. Confusion was total. The French Government had virtually capitulated by asking for an armistice. In charge of the negotiations was Marshall Philippe Pétain, the supposed savior of France at Verdun, a man who was then 84 years old. He had joined the Government May 17 and became Premier June 17. That day he addressed the nation announcing that he was asking for an armistice. He said:

"I offer to France the gift of my person so that I may ease her sorrow. It is with a heavy heart that I tell you that we must halt the combat. Last night I asked the adversary whether he is ready to seek with us, in honor, some way to put an end to the hostilities."

He thought and obviously others thought with him that he could talk to Hitler as an equal, because he was "the Victor of Verdun", hence the honor of France would be safe. He was, of course, completely mistaken for, as head of metropolitan France, he was going to carry out Hitler's diabolical Nazi policies, whether he wanted to or not.

The next day, June 18, the Resistance to the German occupation had already started. The word Resistance was to be heard on the wavelengths of the British Broadcasting Corporation spoken by a newly promoted Brigadier General, Charles de Gaulle, the same man who attempted without success to sell to France the idea that modern war could only be won with armored divisions. Now he was selling to his compatriots the idea that France should continue the battle against the Germans outside the continent along with its Allies. For a few weeks he had been Undersecretary of State and had been in London in early June, having been sent there by Paul Reynaud, then French Premier, to meet with Winston Churchill to discuss the future of France. De Gaulle had come back from that mission the 15th of June and was now in Bordeaux. During the evening of June 16, Churchill received a phone call from General Spears, his personal envoy in France, who reported that the news from France was very bad and that he thought it was better for him to come back to England. He also spoke with some anxiety about the safety of de Gaulle who had expressed to him his desire to continue the fight against the Germans. This political view was not popular with the Pétain government and Churchill gave Spears unrestricted permission to deal with the situation. According to Churchill, on the morning of the 17th, de Gaulle went to his office in Bordeaux, made, as a blind, a number of engagements for the afternoon and then drove to the airfield with his friend Spears to see him off. They shook hands and said good-bye, and as the plane began to move, de Gaulle stepped in and slammed the door. The machine soared off in the air while the French police and official gasped. De Gaulle carried with him, the honor of France. From now on Churchill was to politically and financially support him, for he had recognized early the value of having on his side not only de Gaulle, but also some French troops and part of the mighty French navy .

Here is the appeal of de Gaulle, 18 June at 6P.M.

The leaders who have been at the head of the French armies for many years have formed a government.

This government, alleging the defeat of our armies, has entered into communication with the enemy to stop the fighting.

To be sure, we have been submerged, we are submerged, by the enemy's mechanized forces, on land and in the air.

It is the German tanks, planes and tactics that have made us fall back, infinitely more than their numbers. It is the Germans'tanks, planes and tactics that have so taken our leaders by surprise as to bring them to the point they have reached today.

But has the last word been said? Has all hope gone? Is the defeat final? No. Believe me, I tell you that nothing is lost for France. The same means that beat us may one day bring victory.

For France is not alone. She is not alone! She is not alone! She has an immense empire behind her. She can unite with the British Empire, which commands the sea and which is carrying on with the struggle. Like England, she can make an unlimited use of the vast industries of the United States.

This war is not limited to the unfortunate territory of our country. This war has not been decided by the Battle of France. This war is a world-wide war. All the faults, all the delays, all the sufferings do not do away with the fact that in the world there are all the means for one day crushing our enemies. Today we are struck down by mechanized force; in the future we can conquer by greater mechanized force. The fate of the world lies there.

I, General de Gaulle, now in London, call upon all French officers and soldiers who are on British soil or who may be on it, with their arms or without them, I call upon the engineers and the specialized work-ers in the armaments industry who are or may be on British soil, to get in touch with me.

Whatever happens, the flame of the French Resistance must not and shall not go out.

Tomorrow, as I have done today. I shall speak again from London.

Very few French people heard his appeal, for few of them then ever listened to the BBC which was broadcast in English. Very few read accounts of his message that appeared in several papers in Marseilles and Lyon. But several weeks later everyone in France knew something about de Gaulle and his message which rapidly spread by word of mouth.

De Gaulle believed that it was his duty to save the honor of France for no one else seemed to be ready to do this. The fact that De Gaulle was in England permitted him to pick up the fallen French flag that had been replaced by the Swatiska over France. Against all odds he believed in a victory of the Allies. After all France had an empire and a navy that were

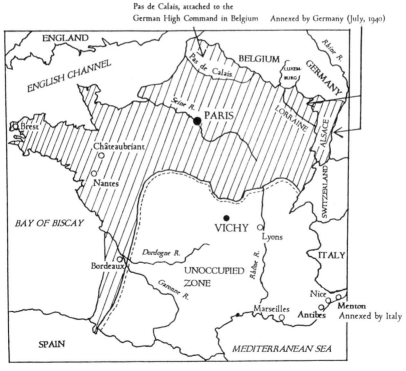

Occupied France—June 1940 - November 1942

not in the hands of the Nazis. France could continue the war.

In his message de Gaulle used the word "resistance" in a conventional military context. But the word was taken up in a broader sense by those who were out of sympathy with defeat and the desire for an armistice. For them it meant a civilian as well as a military fight against Nazi Germany. A few weeks later, multiple embryonic underground networks of resisters, many not associated with de Gaulle or the British, were created by very strong willed people who could not accept the defeat and who were hoping against all odds at the time that in the long run France would be liberated.

On the 25th of June the armistice was signed and France was divided into two zones: a German occupied zone extending from the north of France to as far south as the German troops had gone and a southern non-occupied zone which was to be governed by a French government headed by Marshall Pétain and with the city of Vichy as its capital(see map on preceding page). The two zones were to be separated by a line of demarcation entirely controlled by the German police. The occupied zone, though theoretically subject to the civil government of Vichy, was to be effectively under the control of the Commander-in-chief of the German Army of occupation whose command post was in Paris. Three departments which comprised the provinces of Alsace and Lorraine were annexed by Germany. Every time there was a war between Germany and France the victor got these two provinces. Two departments in the north of France were to be administered by the German High Command in Brussels. This geo-political structure of France remained intact until November 1942 when, in response to the American landing in North Africa, Hitler's troops occupied all France.

PART 2

THE VICHY GOVERNMENT

CHAPTER 3

The Collapse of the Third Republic and the Birth of the Vichy Government

The Collapse of the Third Republic

If America does not intervene you will see France drown herself and disappear after having casted her last look towards the land of liberty from which she was expecting salvation.

PAUL REYNAUD IN A TELEGRAM TO ROOSEVELT.
JUNE 14, 1940

To understand France, it is very important to realize that French people are political animals. There is no doubt in my mind that they take politics as seriously as Americans take baseball. They argue politics constantly. I remember a violent political discussion between Father and his three brothers that took place in 1937 in a town called Vic sur Cère in the middle of France. I forgot the subject of the discussion, but the four brothers managed to have four very different opinions. One of them was arguing his so violently, that he threw his cap at his feet just missing a pile of horse manure. Gilles and I were laughing so hard that we interrupted their conversation as they realized how overheated it had become. Father and his brothers were smiling.

Sometimes it seems that in France there are as many political parties as there are French people. This might explain in part why, contrary to the United States which had the same steady government since 1776, France had many: republics, consulates, empires. There have been three different Republics, each with a different constitution. The First Republic lasted only seven years from 1792 to 1799 when it was replaced by a dictatorship headed by Napoleon Bonaparte who made himself emperor. The second Republic was born in 1848 and died in 1857 as a result of a coup d'état by the nephew of Napoleon, Louis Napoleon Bonaparte. When the latter was defeated by Germany in 1870, France turned again to a Republican form of government and the Third Republic was officially proclaimed in 1875 and lasted until 1940 when France capitulated.

The fall of the Third Republic came in two steps. The first step was the signing of the armistice. The second step was the replacement of a form of republican government by a quasi-fascist dictatorship, since known as the Vichy Government. The armistice came about because most members of the French parliament, physically and emotionally exhausted, did not have the courage, the fortitude and the vision of thirty of their colleagues who were determined to continue the fight against Germany. The latter were a very small minority which at the time appeared foolish, for after all in the summer of 1940 German victory seemed certain. In the complete disarray of the French Government in the last two weeks of June 1940, a minority of Parliamentarians, who wanted to continue the war, boarded a chartered boat out of Bordeaux for North Africa. As soon as they crossed the Mediterranean they were branded as traitors, arrested in Algiers and returned to metropolitan France where they were put in jail by the new government which came into power under Pétain. Two of them, Jean Zay and Georges Mandel, former ministers, were assassinated in 1944.

It is not fair to blame only the French assembly for the capitulation of France and the death of the Third Republic. Its president, Albert Lebrun, and its prime minister, Paul Reynaud, were also responsible. Lebrun, a wishy-washy individual, took too seriously his purely ceremonial duties as president. Forgetting what he symbolized, he allowed himself to be pushed and pulled from all directions, to be tricked by Pierre Laval, one of the most influential of the French deputies, into remaining in France, instead of going to North Africa as he wished to do, and into giving the position of prime minister to Pétain, a man he knew to be very hostile to any form of Republican government.

The character of Paul Reynaud, who had succeeded Daladier March 1940, is harder to figure out than the one of Albert Lebrun. Reynaud was a patriot who had clearly seen the dangers of an ever expanding Germany. He had resigned from the government after Munich. He had an excellent understanding of military affairs. He fought for a better airforce. He realized very early in May that the war on French soil was over. To explore the possibility to continue the fight from a base out of France with the help of the British and possibly the Americans, early in June he sent de Gaulle to London as his representative. Having sacked Gamelin, the inefficient Commander-in-chief of the armed forces, Reynaud nevertheless made a mistake which had serious consequences. He called on two old soldiers of the First World War, Philippe Pétain, who was 84 to be the Deputy Premier and Maxime Weygand who was 73 to replace Gamelin. Both military men were committed defeatists and antiparliamentarians.

For years, as did many French army officers, Weygand viewed the Soviet Union and the French communist party as a graver threat than Nazi Germany. His writings reveal that he had a fairly constant respect for the two fascist states of Italy and Spain. The day before the Germans entered Paris, Weygand, then Commmander-in-chief of the French Forces, told the French Cabinet that he would refuse to leave the soil of France should the Government decide to continue the war in Africa or elsewhere. He also refused to follow Reynaud's directive to seek a purely military capitulation which would leave the French government, like the Dutch, the freedom to carry on the fight from outside the continent. Instead of sacking Weygand for his disobedience, Reynaud stepped down in favor of Pétain who, as the new prime minister, within hours approached the Germans for an armistice.

It is hard to understand why Reynaud called on two men who did not share his political and military views. His behavior seemed to have been more erratic than his thinking, for he is reported to have said to his ministers at the time: "You believe that you are coming to an understanding with Hitler. You think that he is an old gentleman like "Guillaume I" who took two provinces from you and then life began again. You are mistaken. Hitler is Genghis Khan."

It has been said that Reynaud's strength of character had been sapped at the time by the irrational demands of his mistress, the Countess Helène des Portes, while France was being run over by German armor. This might have been true, but it is also true that he was terribly ill-advised and even lied to by his entourage, particularly concerning military conditions. Most of the people surrounding him, including the Countess, were looking no further ahead than to an immediate peace which seemed at the time to be the most rational thing to do. Resistance to Germany looked foolish for her victory over England seemed certain.

Sad to say, the French government reflected the almost unanimous public opinion. France was stunned, shocked, despaired, and was crying for peace. In that summer of 1940 total confusion was the rule.

In the summer of 1940, France was physically and economically paralyzed. Six million French citizens were still on the roads waiting to go back home. Everywhere food was scarce, not because there was not any, but because it could not be transported where it was needed. Trains, trucks, and buses, were not running. People had no money left and there was not any in the local government coffers to help them out. People who stayed in their homes in the cities found themselves without gas, water, and food. Except for the segment of the population which worked on farms, French people found themselves without work because factories had shut down and shops had closed. Everything was at a standstill. Administrators of social institutions had let go their mental patients and children from orphanages to roam the streets. The French turned to the occupation army for help. They did not get much. They now welcomed a government, any type of government, that could reestablish some normalcy to everyday life.

There was also moral confusion for no one admitted responsibility for the defeat. Everyone blamed someone else. Ordinary soldiers blamed their officers. The General Staff blamed the politicians. The politicians of the right blamed those of the left and vice versa. Every one blamed the communists who in turn blamed the French fascists who blamed the Jews. Few blamed the Germans for starting the war in the first place. A military armistice was demanded, and enforced, imposed by Weygand and Pétain on two broken French leaders, Reynaud and Lebrun, who threw up their hands not able to imagine that within a few days the strictly military armistice would lead to a semi- coup d'état which would suppress the basic laws of the Republic. In other words the military High Command took over the French civil government. The third Republic had ended. A new government was born.

The Birth of the Vichy Government

Moreover, it is necessary to know what we mean by to follow the Vichy Government. At first it was everyone. At the end it was nobody.

CHARLES DE GAULLE

After sixty years, France has been delivered from the yoke of the radical and anti-catholic party (professors, lawyers, Jews and Freemasons). The new government is invoking God and restoring the Grande Chartreuse to the religious orders. There is hope that we may be delivered from universal suffrage and parliamentarism; and also from the evil and imbecile domination of the school teachers who covered themselves with shame in the last war. Authority is restored.

PAUL CLAUDEL (1868-1955)

In 1940 and for many years after that I thought that the Vichy Government came to power as a result of an illegal coup d'état. However, as I found years later, this was not exactly the case. It came to power because on July 9 the members of the parliament gave up their constitutional rights to govern France and entrusted Marshal Pétain with the job. The next day they proposed that the constitution of 1875 be suspended and that Pétain be granted full powers to establish the bases of a new constitution. This turn of affairs came about as a result of weakness, despair, and pure treason on the part of those who had been elected by the French people.

But, if it can be argued that there was a need for an armistice to restore the civil government and reestablish some normalcy to French society, nothing obliged the French to change their form of government. The Germans had not asked them to do this. And even if there had been a need to do so, why not wait until cooler heads prevailed and why give the job to Marshall Pétain, then 84 years old, who could die any day? In fact he died in prison in 1951 seven years after the liberation of France.

It seems that the Vichy Government came into being as a result of political intrigues and underhanded dealings. The original and main players were two deputies, Pierre Laval and Raphael Alibert, who soon became members of Pétain's government. They were the first to think of using the defeat of France to overthrow the Third Republic which they both hated, but for different reasons. Alibert was a convinced monarchist who was determined to destroy any Republican government and restore the monarchy. It is harder to understand the motives of Laval who at one time was a socialist. However, we know that he firmly believed that Germany would win the war and that all Europe was to be under the Nazi boot for a long time. It was evident to him that France should adapt to the Hitlerian order, and the sooner the better. According to him a republican form of government was an obstacle to this objective. Both men forced their views on their parliamentary colleagues. They lied, they threatened, and they succeeded in having the French Assembly consent to abandon their power and sacrifice liberty in the conviction that a new regime would be better in restoring order and bringing a more lenient peace with Hitler.

To be fair to Laval and Alibert, it has to be said that they did not have to do much to persuade the French assembly to commit suicide on July 9th. They did not create the mood of national self-recrimination in which the assembly gathered in Vichy on that day when it voted to give full powers to Pétain including the power to revamp the constitution of 1875. For the deputies and senators who were present the humiliation of the total defeat translated itself in a madness of self-flagellation. For them it was France itself which was in great part responsible for its own disaster and instead of blaming the defeat on the superiority of the German forces they blamed it on the constitution of the Third Republic which they decided had to be changed. For some obscure reason they confused the form of government with its membership. If a boat runs aground because the crew is incompetent, you do not destroy the boat, you refloat it with the idea of changing the crew. France had lost a battle. It had not yet lost he war.

It ran aground, but it could have been refloated with a new crew of ministers who could easily have continued the war. Instead, the French assembly scuttled the boat by giving Pétain full powers not only to rule France during the period of the Armistice days, but to draft a new constitution.

But in fact, this new constitution was never prepared, or if it was, it was never submitted for approval by the French people. Instead, by fiat, as a good army officer, Pétain consolidated all legislative and executive power in his own hands, substituting a dictatorial government for the Third Republic and even named his successor. He firmly believed that this substitution would forever eliminate what he called the chaos of parliamentary squabbles, the plotting and intrigues of the politicians that resulted in a game of ministerial musical chairs. Pétain believed that this political maneuvering had been responsible for the shameful defeat and the present tragic state of the French people. It seemed that he had forgotten that he had been a part of that problem for he had been the war minister for many months in a Republican government that he now abhored.

In 1940-41 millions of Frenchmen accepted the Vichy Government. It is not difficult to understand why. They were physically and emotionally exhausted, anxious to come back home to some normal activity. Their main preoccupation was now with getting food. Furthermore, their political conscience was at a low ebb, for they were bombarded daily by a defeatist propaganda of lies coming from Vichy radio, newspapers and cinema newsreels. Freedom of the press had been completely suppressed. Some believed that Pétain was playing a double game. They thought that he would call for armed resistance when the right day came. But he never did.

The turning point of public opinion came at the end of 1942. As the war dragged on and as the Vichy government slid more and more down the road towards fascism, it became evident to many of the French people that they had bet on the wrong horse. A large number of them changed camps starting to help the resisters and saving the lives of the enemies of Vichy. This switch of positions was hard for me to understand at the time. When we are young, we have a tendency to see everything in black and white; to divide people into good guys and bad guys. So for me, a boy of fifteen in 1940, the people who were fighting the Germans were the good guys, the people who collaborated with them were the bad guys. How come good guys could become bad guys and vice- versa. Later I found that, human nature being complex, my view of this period had been simplistic. Reasons for the switch could be understood in terms of a hunger for power or self-preservation in the face of a changing war.

Like my parents I never accepted Vichy as the legitimate government, possibly because I never trusted it. I found later that I was completely right in my judgment. Vichy was a fascist government, not simply a puppet government. To deny that to a great extent it was hamstrung by the German presence would be to assign a false autonomy to Vichy that it never had, yet its hands were never completely tied either. Its freedom to deal with internal affairs was considerable. However, instead of using it to counteract German policies, it carried out its own policy of fascism.

Completely on its own, and very early, the Vichy Government arrested, imprisoned, and in some cases assassinated resisters, Gaullists, communists, and politicians of the Third Republic who had opposed its establishment. On its own, and very early, it removed freemasons, socialists, and Jews from public office. Independently from the Nazis, it interned Jews, men, women, and children in concentration camps, at first those who were not born in France, then later also those who were. It was not the Nazis who ransacked the synagogue of Nice, but French antisemites, as the French police stood close-by in apathy or connivance. Vichy did not just carry out the orders of the German government, it anticipated them and went beyond them. Instead of saving its citizens from the wrath of Hitler, as the Danish Government did, it helped the Germans to carry out their programs. This continued even after D-Day. Probably the best evidence for the complicity of the Vichy government with the Nazis was its willingness to select hostages to be shot by the Germans. It should have left the process solely to Germans so that they would have been responsible for the deaths of so many Frenchmen.

The men of Vichy were persuaded that the war could end only in the victory of Germany. They conceived their role to be one of satisfying the victor until after England's defeat when a reasonable peace treaty could be expected as payment for their obliging posture. They believed that Hitler would be more lenient in his peace terms if France gave evidence that it felt it had sinned and started a new life of repentance. However, they did not understand, or did not want to know, what such victory meant: the complete rule of Hitler over Europe, a complete colonization of that continent by his henchmen. At first, they attempted a politics of reconciliation with the Germans which translated into a collaboration, but Hitler was not the least interested in any reconciliation. He wanted total collaboration from the French and his objective was annihilation of his adversaries. Later, the men of Vichy found to their childish dismay that collaboration leads to more collaboration and finally to slavery. Like the proverbial ostriches, they buried their heads in the sand, but this sand was quick sand into which their whole bodies soon sunk.

To those who later affirmed that Vichy had saved France, it is hard on material grounds to know whether the fate of France without Vichy would have been worse. It is true that the problems France faced in June 1940 were staggering and the armistice permitted millions of refugees to slowly return to their homes. But it did little to bring back home from

Germany the two million war prisoners who composed much of the French work force, and to restore family life. The Vichy government did nothing to prevent the looting of France by the Germans, who for four years stole food and coal and all the necessary things of modern civilization. It also did nothing to prevent the annexation of Alsace-Lorraine by Germany. Finally, on military grounds, if France had continued the war from its bases in its colonial empire, it would have facilitated the task of the Allies and it is highly possible that their victory would have come sooner.

On moral grounds it is easy to argue that the fate of France without Vichy would have been better. The Vichy government followed at best a policy of waiting to see where the wind blows. At its worse its policy of intensive collaboration brought the disarray of the country, setting the French against the French. It encouraged an official collaboration of thousands of French people in carrying out the most abject crimes against humanity. Denunciation by Frenchmen and arrest by Frenchmen became the rule. Without French traitors the Gestapo would have achieved far fewer arrests. Without Vichy the victimization of communists, freemasons, and teachers might not have existed. As far as the victimization of the Jews is concerned, it would have occurred, but it would not have been so intense, for fewer Jews would have been identified and more would have been saved by their countrymen. On the other hand, the odious persecution of the Jews on the part of Vichy created a backlash within the French population that deepened the social and political conflict, and strengthened the ideological opposition to Vichy in a passionate struggle for basic human values.

Without Vichy, the French would not have been misled into believing that their government was working for them, when in fact it was not and could not. Without Vichy, the nation would not have been fooled by words of government officers whose actions were in direct contradiction of what they were saying. Without Vichy, there would have been, of course, a collaborationist government, but its members would have been recruited from a very small minority of frenzied French Nazis, a government similar to the one in Norway. Without Vichy, it would have been easier for the Resistance to recruit its members from a unified population.

To be fair, one has to say that not all the men of the Vichy Government were perfect collaborators. From time to time some of them attempted to resist, for example, by approaching in vain the Allies in secret negotiations, or by negotiating with the Germans, trying to get them to decrease their demands. But the French population never knew about this. All they heard were the official speeches of Pétain, Darlan, and Laval who preached collaboration with the Germans. It is interesting to note that in 1940 the Vichy Government did not realize the power of the radio, in particular the British and the Swiss, whose French broadcasts counteracted the lies of Vichy and Berlin. Technology was already changing the way wars and politics were to be perceived by the people involved—the way, thirty years later, that television would bring the Vietnam war into the living rooms of American homes.

For Pétain, the defeat of France had not been caused by the imeptitude of the military, of which he was a part, but a lack of moral valor on the part of the French nation. It was time for bringing a "moral" revolution within the French population. According to Pétain suffering engenders valor. Out of misfortune is born salvation. To stimulate human energy, nothing is better than suffering." In 1940, the spirit of enjoyment had to be replaced by the spirit of sacrifice. It was time to purify and strengthen the national fiber. It was time for discipline for the parents as well as their children. Family ties were to be strengthened; marriages were to be harder to break and mothers were to stay home. School teachers were to be the ones to create this new species of man, "homo nationalis." They were not only to teach students scientific and humanistic knowledge, but also to instill a sense of duties owed to the French State, to give them respect for the law (which Pétain did not seem to have) and to develop patriotic feelings towards France. Furthermore, the teachers were to talk to the students about God, something which was not done in Republican schools. Well, unfortunately for Pétain, nothing really concrete came out of this national revolution.

Chapter 4

Vichy And The Jews

The statues of the Virgin Mary and infant Jesus disappeared from Notre Dame Cathedral. Upon being questioned the sacristan explained that they had gone to the nearest police station . "They had to register as Jews."

SOME HUMOR IN PARIS IN 1941

The first antisemitic measures taken by Vichy occurred as early as October 1940, months before the Germans required them. The Vichy government, the most virulent racist regime that ever ruled France, had its own policy of antisemitism which involved four phases: first, identification of the Jews; second, expropriation of their properties; third, gathering them in concentration camps and fourth, delivering them to the Gestapo which murdered them.

Identification of French Jews for the Vichy Government was not simple, because, contrary to the customs of other countries such as Poland, they did not live in ghettoes. Since the early 18th century they had enjoyed the same rights as other French citizens and lived among them. They adopted their mode of dress and French as their mother tongue. They took advantage of the educational opportunities offered by the successive governments at a faster rate than the population at large, securing economic and social mobility for their children who considered themselves completely French. With time, there was a decline in religious practice and an increase in the number of marriages between "Jews" and non-Jews. Many intellectuals among them had abandoned religious observance and severed their ties to the ethnic community. They felt neither pride nor shame in their origins. They simply became intellectually and nationally French. For them Judaism was one of those religions that some French practice and some not. All this helps to explain why Zionism never took hold in France. It is interesting to note that for years very few foreign Jews came to France, possibly because for them France was either too Catholic or too anticlerical and there was no real Jewish community to receive them for shelter and support. It is only with the excesses of Nazi antisemitism that there was a sudden influx of foreign Jews into France from Eastern Europe and Germany. These immigrants were easily identified, because they formed a unified community separate from the French Jews whose assimilation and acculturation had progressed so far that they could not be distinguished from the rest of the population unless, in some way, they identified themselves as Jews.

So, in order to isolate the French Jews from the rest of the French citizens, the Vichy Government had to define who was a Jew and then issue a decree that forced "Jews" to register. The Vichy definition of who as a Jew transcended the Nazi definition as it applied in Germany or in occupied France.

According to Berlin, a "Jew" was anyone with at least three Jewish grand parents, or someone who had two Jewish grand parents and who belonged to the Jewish religious community. Someone who had two Jewish grandparents and who was not affiliated with the Jewish religious community and who was not married to a Jew, was not considered a "Jew", but a Mischling first degree. If someone had only one Jewish grandparent, he or she was considered a Mischling second degree. But according to Vichy, someone who had only two Jewish grandparents was considered a "Jew." Children of a Jew and a non-Jew were considered Jews. Since under the Vichy statutes the number of Jewish grandparents required to make someone a Jew was reduced to two, persons who escaped the German anti-Jewish measures in the occupied zone because they only had two Jewish grand parents were branded as *Jews* if they happened to be in the unoccupied zone. In less than two years these definitions of who was a Jew became of extreme importance since they determined who was to live or die.

Once Vichy had defined, who was a Jew its next step was to register them. When identified, Jews would be prevented from occupying any position of public influence, be excluded from participation in the press, radio, cinema and theater. Only a few would be permitted to practice medicine, and or teach at universities. It has been reported that Pétain had insisted that no Jew should be a judge or a teacher.

Not only did the Jews have to register, they also had to declare their financial holdings. The official reason for doing this was to eliminate all Jewish influence from the national economy." But, in fact it was done to dispossess them. To accomplish this Vichy issued another decree in June 1941, similar to those issued in Germany, which permitted the enterprises belonging to Jews or run by them to be taken away from them without compensation. These enterprises were to be administered by non-Jews chosen for their political views, not for their business sense. This expropriation was referred to as the Aryanization of French business. Under the Vichy government the Jewish population was completely deprived of its economic rights, as it was under the Nazi government.

Who was to have the property taken from the Jews became a real struggle between the Nazis and Vichy, especially when it concerned art. Both rushed to snatch private collections from private homes and museums in occupied France. Among the most notorious "art lovers" were Alfred Rosenberg, the Nazi theoretician and Herman Goring, the chief of the Lutwaffe. Even Pétain did not seem to see anything wrong with the idea of robbing Jews, for he wanted to give to the Spanish Government a fresco of the Spanish painter, Jose-Maria Sert, which was hanging in the chateau of Laversine owned by a member of the Rothschild family. He seemed to have shared with Rosenberg the idea that Jews have no rights.

In order to help in setting the Jews apart, Vichy created two governmental organizations. The first one was a Bureau of Jewish Affairs which opened its doors on March 1941. The second bureau that Vichy created was L' Union Générale des Israélites Français (U.G.I.F.) which was set up two months later.

The purpose of the Bureau of Jewish Affairs was to implement the already existing decrees with regard to the Jews, to propose further legislations needed in order to supervise the liquidation of Jewish property and enforce these decrees by force if necessary. Its first head was Xavier Vallat, an avowed antisemite. He was reported to have said to his employees: "A Jew must be called a Jew and not described in writing as Mr.Levy or Mr.Dreyfus, but as the *Jew Levy* or *the Jew Dreyfus*." It was Vallat and the French police, not the Gestapo, that carried out to perfection the policy of locating and counting the Jews in the occupied zone. To detect who was a Jew, Vallat suggested looking up in registry offices first names such as Abraham, Aaron, etc. for men, and Sarah, Ruth, etc. for women. As far as last names were concerned, one should look them up in Jewish cemeteries. If one were to follow Vallat's advice in the United States, Abraham Lincoln would have been arrested and deported to a death camp. Vallat considered himself to be a serious antisemite of long standing. He is reported to have said to an S.S. officer: "I have been an antisemite far longer than you." Yet, his antisemitism was not strong enough for the Nazis who found him too slow and too independent. One year after his appointment he was replaced by Darquier de Pellepoix. In de Pellepoix, a venomous racist, the Nazis found the man they needed, a man who collaborated with them completely in the mass deportation of the Jews to Eastern Europe. Ironically, he was replaced by Mercier du Paty de Clam, a man whose heart was with the Resistance. De Clam used his authority to disorganize the administration of the Bureau of Jewish Affairs. This case was not unique. Unknown to the S.S., a Jew had infiltrated their ranks and managed to be second in command of the deportation of Jews from occupied France. He successfully warned many of them that they were going to be arrested, permitting them to escape the holocaust.

The history of the U.G.I.F is a very sad one. The Red Cross never helped the Jews in distress. This role fell on the shoulders of the U.G.I.F, which had been established officially for that purpose by the Germans. This welfare organization run by Jews alleviated some of the suffering and was instrumental in saving many lives especially those of children. However, the real objective of the establishment of UGIF by the Nazis was to set the Jews definitely apart, to levy tremendous fines upon them, and in the end to permit the French police and the Gestapo to locate, arrest, and murder them, including the executive board of the U.G.I.F and its employees who perished in concentration camps.

There is no doubt that the Vichy anti-semitic decrees of 1940 and 1941 made it much easier for the Nazis to carry out the "final solution." In fact, after the war, they admitted that without the census [of the Jews] they would have been tremendously handicapped in carrying out Hitler's orders for extermination of the Jews living in France. Some people have attempted to defend Vichy's actions by affirming that the Jews in unoccupied France were treated far better than those in occupied France. To support this idea they rightly stated that Jews under Vichy never wore the yellow star and that the Vichy government made a distinction between French and Foreign Jews. This last assertion was only partly correct. It is true that the distinction between Foreign and French Jews was always present in the mind of Laval who considered the Jewish problem from a nationalist point of view. He was perfectly willing to abandon the Foreign

Jews to Hitler, but not the French Jews whom he considered to be perfectly assimilated. Yet at the end he also abandoned them to the Nazis for political concessions. Throughout 1940 and 1944 France had the worse antisemitic government of all Europe except Germany and Bulgaria. Even Hungary, an ally of Hitler, was two years behind France in persecuting its own Jewish citizens.

The way Vichy treated the Foreign Jews was a complete disgrace. By two decrees in October 1940, it allowed the prefect of each department to find foreign Jews and transfer them from wherever they were living to "special camps." The most notable camp, Gurs, near the Spanish border in the department of the Basses Pyrenées, became a byword for inhumanity and suffering. A few died there and most of these Foreign Jews, including their French born children, were later delivered to the Nazis and exterminated. Among them were some men who had just fought in the war side by side with French soldiers. Such treatment of human beings aroused the general indignation of the French population, including some representatives of the Catholic and Protestant Churches. The Catholic Church hierarchy itself found its own breaking point with the brutal round up of children in the summer of 1942, but did mot do much to alleviate their condition. The Vichy Government delivered to the Nazis not only Jews, but Gypsies. For some reason, it did not officially discriminate against Blacks. As a matter of fact, one of its own minister was "black."

PART 3

HEAVEN ON EARTH

CHAPTER 5

Our Home Before The War

If Cannes is the pearl of the Riviera, Menton is the pearl of France.

AN OLD SAYING

When Father decided to retire in 1932, he and Mother looked for a place to live on the French Riviera of which they had fond memories. They had lived for a few months in 1916 in the region between Hyères and Fréjus, when Father was recuperating from having been gassed during the war. The region, called "Les Maures", is named after the Moors who had occupied this land centuries ago. It is a massif of round mountains, rising in

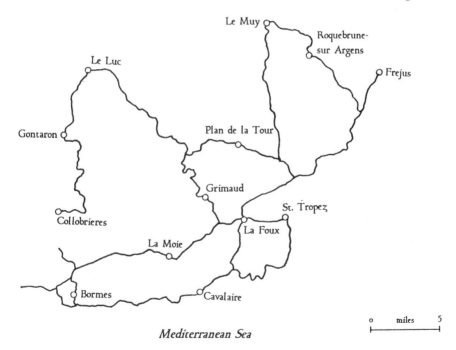

**Les Maures, part of the French Riviera,
where our parents passed a few months in 1916 after our father
had been gassed.**

places to 2,555 feet in height, which are scooped out into valleys that
descend rapidly to the sea and to little bays. The convex coast line is
exposed to all the fury of southerly and eastern winds, but quite protected
from the mistral, the north-west wind which often blows when the sky is
clear and the sun warm. Hence, the bays afford shelter from cold winter
winds, permitting the date palms to ripen their fruits, and protecting the
eucalyptuses and the oranges from frost. The lower slopes have many olive
trees and vines, and all kinds of flowering shrubs, lavender, lentiscus, myrtle, arbutus and pomegranates. The higher land is covered with many different types of trees, dark chestnuts, pines, carubs and cork oaks. The latter have led to a local industry of cork manufacturing. In many places one
can see oak trunks peeled bare of their barks, which have been pried off in
a single sheet, leaving the limbs completely naked of the substance which
most of us regard as a growth peculiar to bottle necks.

This isolated part of the Riviera played an important part during World
War II. It was here that English submarines surfaced for a few moments
to pick up or deliver important political people or underground agents. It
was also here that in August of 1944 American and French troops landed
to liberate Southern France.

The little shy town in Les Maures where Father and Mother stayed during World War I was called Cavalaire. It was at the time served by a small
railway on a single track which meandered through the woods. Mother
used to tell stories about the only train that came once a day across Les
Maures. At every station the engineer used to deliver all kinds of things
that the local inhabitants had asked him to buy at Toulon, from nails to
women's panties. Cavalaire was so quiet and sunny, with the fragrance of
all kinds of wild flowers, that it seemed to be thousands of miles from
Verdun, one of the bloodiest battlefronts that ever existed. One day Father
saw a gamekeeper in an odd uniform with fieldglasses sprawled over a
large branch of a maritime pine that overlooked the beach. "What are you
doing? " asked Father. "I am looking for German submarines." The gamekeeper answered. "This is a dangerous job, you know." Father left the
gamekeeper wondering how many submarines had ever crossed the
Mediterranean sea throughout the war and what the chances were that anyone of them could have been seen from the seashore through fieldglasses.

Sixteen years later my parents first looked for a home around Saint
Tropez. They found a nice place they liked, but decided against locating
there because Gilles and I would have had a long trek to school. They

judged that Saint Tropez was too far from real civilization. They could not predict that years later Saint Tropez would become one of the most world famous places for the jet set, rivaling Cannes.

They then looked around Monaco. One day Mother found the place of her dreams. Standing in front of a beautiful wooden gate without even entering the premises, she turned to Father and said: "Maurice, this is it." They bought it that day and never regretted doing so. I understand perfectly why Mother immediately fell in love with this place. The double hinged wooden gate, anchored by two graceful pillars which were flanked by two large cypresses, opened up into a long grape arbor walkway. This beautiful walkway led to a large house surrounded by palm and orange trees. To her right, Mother could see the quiet blue Mediterranean sea, and in front of her the high mountains dropping precipituously into the sea.

France is divided into departments which themselves are divided into communes (counties). Our new home was in the commune of Roquebrune-Cap Martin in the Department of Alpes Maritimes. The department got its name from the fact that the Alps, gigantic grey massifs, rise almost straight out of the sea. Our villa, for every villa on the French Riviera has a name, was appropriately called Clair Matin or Clear Morning: one morning was so clear that we were able to see, for the first time the outline of the island of Corsica lying off to the east about 80 miles away.

The commune of Roquebrune-Cap Martin has at least three distinct parts: the old village of Roquebrune perched 800 feet above the sea, the Cap Martin peninsula with its rocky shore fringed by pine trees, and the commercial district of Carnolès, which lies to the west and is separated from Menton by a bridge, the Pont de l'Union, across the small Gorbio river. The rest of the commune of Roquebrune-Cap Martin is made up of the lower slopes of the mountains between Menton and Monte Carlo, consisting of terraces sustained by non-cemented walls built long ago by the inhabitants of the region. These non-cemented walls must be repaired occasionally, an art transmitted from one generation to the next, and one that I acquired as a young teenager from a colorful old man, named Fratini. Fratini worked fast and well when he was not inebriated. Drinking red wine was his downfall. Whenever someone told him that he would not go to heaven because he drank too much, he used to answer: "Saint Peter will let me in, for they need someone to weed God's gardens."

It is rather easy to make a stone wall with cement. After all the stones do not need to fit exactly against each other, for pouring cement between stones hides any flaw. Making a stone wall without cement, on the other hand, is a real challenge. It requires special skills: how to chose stones meshing exactly and how to imagine special niches where these stones will fit. Large stones have to be laid first slightly sloping towards the inside of the wall. Yet the wall has to be kept vertical. Any cavity between the large stones has to be filled with small ones that have to fit exactly. The only useful tool is a hammer for breaking a piece of stone which is in the way of a better fit. Picking up a stone and seeing where it fits in the pattern of the wall is the key to success. In other words stone walling (no pun intended) requires the eye of an architect and Old Fratini had one.

This wiry old man used to eat at noon, as most agricultural workers in the region did, a panbagna. In the local dialect, pan means bread and bagna means bathed, but this regional sandwich is not bathed in water, but in virgin olive oil. To make a panbagna you cut a loaf of French bread lengthwise in two parts. You then lay slices of juicy, red tomatoes full of A and D vitamins, a few black anchovies, and a few slices of onion or garlic on the top of one of the half loaves. Then, you pour enough olive oil on the top of all this so that the oil soaks the bread, but does not go through the crust. You replace the other half of the loaf and eat his large sandwich with two hands, preferably sitting outside with your head slightly bent and your knees separated from each other in order to prevent the dripping oil from staining your clothes. From time to time, remembering my youth on the French Riviera, I prepare a panbagna and eat it with a smile, for I have known for a long time that such a sandwich does marvels for your health. I instinctively knew what has been recently confirmed, that vegetables, and especially olive oil, contain something that lowers one's cholesterol and reduces the chances for heart attacks. What particular ingredient in olive oil is beneficial we do not know as yet.

The old village of Roquebrune extends along a spur of the mountain with precipices on two sides. To reach the village by car one drives up a winding road that leads to the entrance of the village, a square, called Place des Frères. It is impossible to drive inside the village itself because of its narrow winding mule-step, steep streets around which the old and quaint, but colorful houses crowd together often hewn out of the puddingstone in vaults.

Roquebrune has a long history as it existed before the arrival of the Romans. At one time it belonged to the Count of Ventimiglia, and was sold by him in 477 to a Genoese family called Ventos. In 1189 it fell into the hands of the Lascaris family until around 1353 when Carlo Grimaldi of Monaco bought the town from Gugliemo Lascaris, uniting Monaco, Roquebrune, and Menton for nearly 500 years. Then, in 1848, the populations of Menton and Roquebrune rebelled against the Grimaldi and declared themselves Republics, remaining as such until they were united with France in 1860.

At the top of the village there is a 10th century castle, the Chateau de Lascaris, built to fight the Saracens. It is a good representative of a medieval fortress, with a fine, square tower still standing among the ruins that date from 1560 after the Turks had sacked it. In front of the castle are

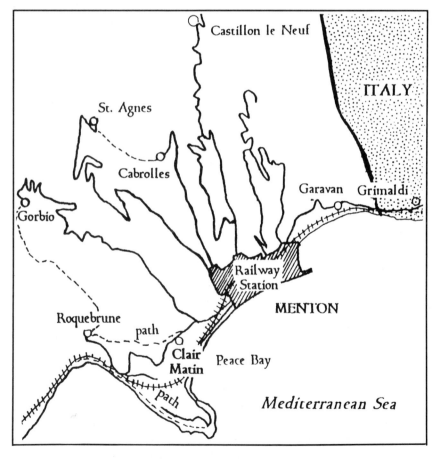

Menton and its surroundings

the advance defences, now skillfully covered with flower beds. The castle can be visited and as a small boy it was a pleasure for me to bring family friends to see it, because if the guide was not there, which was often, I gave them tours of the castle telling the stories and the jokes that the guide would have told. Unfortunately, I do not remember any of them today.

There is a legend that the village of Roquebrune and the castle stood a little higher up than they do now, but that one night the whole of it slipped down to its present site, so that when the villagers awoke in the morning they found themselves down the slope. There could be some truth to this since there are ruins higher up which could be part of the old village. It is likely that the slipping might have been due to heavy rains or the result of an earthquake which occurs from time to time in this region. The legend led to an interesting and colorful festival, la Fête des genets, held during the month of June. It is believed that the genets, rugged shrubs with powerful soil-penetrating roots, were planted on the hills to prevent further slipping. Whatever grain of truth there may be in this, the official reason of the festival is to bless the presence of the genets whose main function is indeed to hold the village onto the mountain, but who needs a reason for a festival anyway!

A second festival that attracts many tourists on the first Sunday in August every year commemorates the end of an epidemic plague which ravaged the area until August 5, 1467. There is a procession in which living tableaux represent scenes from the Passion in all the picturesqueness of a faithful historical reconstruction, with the glitter and color of costumes and uniforms. The actors are all natives of Roquebrune, and the different roles descend from father to son.

To reach the old village from our house our friends had a twenty minute walk on a dirt footpath through extensive olive groves. These trees had a great charm, with their venerable age and dark rugged trunks contrasting sharply with their small, light silvery, grey-green foliage, waving gracefully about with every light breeze. But the most interesting things to be found were the wild herbs growing there: myrtle, rosemary, sage, terragon, thyme, laurel, and lavender. Many of them are used in provincial cooking and Mother never bought any for she could get all what she needed a few hundred feet from our property. It was a real pleasure to take that foot path to go to the village of Roquebrune. Today it is gone, sadly replaced by a freeway, a victim of what has been called progress.

Though the hills above Clair Matin were rich with wild plants and crickets which chirped all through the spring nights, they had, to the despair of the local hunters, no blackbirds, partridges, or rabbits. Yet, from time to time, especially on Sunday afternoons, we could hear gunshots. Were they local hunters shooting their own caps, like the famous hunters of the illustrious town of Tarascon, north of Marseilles? No, they were mostly shooting at lizards and small snakes. I think they were also on the lookout for the legendary tournepatte. The tournepatte is a local bird whose right leg is shorter than its left, due to the fact that it is always sitting on the same side of the hill, facing south to enjoy the sun. Once you have located a tournepatte it is very easy to get him. All you have to do is to imitate the sound of a gunshot. The terrified bird turns around and since it has one leg shorter than the other he falls on his head. All that is left to do is to pick it up.

The hills were so dry in the summer that the thinest sparkle from a cigarette butt falling into a thicket or from a lone lighting bolt could touch off a blaze that the wind would fan to gigantic proportions. I still remember fighting with other volunteers one of these spectacular fires in 1946 by shoveling dirt on the flames, for we had no access to water.

Cap Martin, the other part of the name of the commune, is a limestone promontory to the west of the town of Menton. Its name comes from "Campus Martius" after a camp that the Romans had there. Cap Martin has an extremely rocky shore with many parasol pines ringing it. It was a favorite site for the residences of royalty and the millionaires of Europe. Beautiful villas with well-laid out gardens fringe the western shore, overlooking Monte Carlo and Monaco. Here the ex-Empress Eugenie, wife of Napoleon III, spent the last winters of her life and also where the last King of Montenegro died in 1921.

Between the cape and the old town of Roquebrune the steep sides of the hills are fastooned with beautiful yellow washed, green shuttered and red roofed villas standing in well tended gardens. Along the Eastern shore of the Cape is a level, shady walk and drive lying beneath pine trees and giving a beautiful panorama of Menton and even of the Italian side as far as Bordighera. This is the drive frequented by lovers in horse-drawn carriages, immortalized in the famous film, "The Red Shoes."

Menton is the last town on the road to Italy. It has been said that its flowers and gardens make it the bouquet of the Riviera. It is such a charming place that according to a local legend it was here that Adam and Eve, chased from the earthly paradise, chose to stop after walking through cold mountains and over sun-scorched plains. The legend claims that it was in Menton where Eve planted her golden fruit, not an apple but a lemon, and since then lemon trees grow luxuriantly on the slopes of Menton. Well, perhaps Menton was not the cradle of the first human couple, but it apparently was for some prehistoric men and women, for their skeletal remains, found in 1872, are evidence that they lived in the caves of the Red Rocks situated at the border. These remains are on display in a small museum.

Menton lies in an amphitheater of mountains rising one above the other, thus closing it off for the most part from the Tramontane and Mistral, the cold winds from the North. Being one of the warmest places on the French Riviera, plants grow marvelously well— olive trees reach gigantic heights, palm trees and cacti can be found in many private and public gardens, and Menton is the only place in France where lemon trees can freely fruit. The lemon variety that grows here flowers throughout the year without resting, flower and fruit being on the tree at the same time. But there are no ancient lemon trees, as about once in every thirty years a bitter winter sets in and the old trees perish. The streets of the town are lined with orange and lemon trees, the latter creating a large industry which is celebrated each spring by the town residents with, yes, another festival that is very similar to Mardi-Gras. That week the central square, le Jardin de Biovès, opposite the Casino, is laid out in a series of parterres decorated with lemons and carnations that growers bring to exhibit.

The harbor, full of fishing boats, is deep enough to shelter large ships. It has a lighthouse at the entrance and a sea wall and parapet 50 feet high and 450 yards long. It offers a splendid view of the Pont St. Louis and the Rochers Rouges, a small promontory of red rocks which forms the frontier between France and Italy. The harbor divides the town of Menton into two parts, the West Bay, Menton proper with the old town, and the East Bay, called Garavan.

The mountains behind Garavan appear to make an impregnable wall, but deep within them lie the small, old grey towns of Peille, Contes, Gorbio, Ste. Agnes, Castillon, and Castellar. Within four narrow valleys running into the hills, four streams find their way down to the sea, the Gorbio, the Borrigo, the Caret and the Fossan.

The old town of Menton is highly picturesque with its painted houses, each one rising above another, and crowned by the Church of Saint Michel. Following World War II musical concerts have taken place back of the Church, for the acoustics there are extraordinary. There is also an old market, not much used anymore. Along the narrow streets with mule steps small shops are supplied with provisions of all sorts. Just beyond the town, eastward, is the Chalet des Rosiers which was occupied by Queen Victoria in the Spring of 1883. The memory of her presence there was recognized in April 1939 by the unveiling of her statue at the harbor. The coming of English visitors in Menton is primarily due to the writings of a certain Dr. Henry Bennet, who loved the town and praised its charm and delightful sunny winters. Famous English authors wrote some of their masterpieces in Menton. Among them were Katherine Mansfield and John Richard Green. Green was buried here, and on his tombstone are inscribed the words: "He died learning."

Compared to Nice or Cannes further west, Menton was, and still is, a sleepy very friendly town with its shops' doors ajar to invite you in. Menton has only two drawbacks. Although the Mediterranean Sea is practically tideless, it is far from being still and sometimes can get rough enough to hurl pebbles onto the top of the beaches. In addition, Menton and its surroundings are the only places in France where earthquakes occur, though not frequently. In our first month living here, a tidal wave struck one night, hurling rocks into parts of the town and damaging it rather extensively. The following day, we considered that we might have made a mistake by moving from Paris to the French Riviera, but we stayed, for here the sun shines most of the time, except for sudden and brief storms which can soak one to the skin in a matter of minutes. Fortunately, the rain never lasts long.

Clair Matin, our spacious villa, was located in the center of a flower farm extending over 15 acres. It was a beautiful place in the terraced hills just above Carnoles, which administratively depended on the commune of Roquebrune-Cap Martin, but was attached to Menton economically. Our house, still standing today, overlooked the blue Mediterranean sea and the Gorbio valley. To reach the house we had to either climb on foot 99 steps from the base of the steep hill or drive up a private road with four sharp hairpins.

The 99 cemented steps snaked through the hill, which was sprinkled with a few houses and was covered with pines, oaks, carub trees and wild shrubs that gave their original fragrance. Going down the hill was no problem. But climbing it was no picnic, especially when we were carrying our school books or a few groceries. Father used to get the heavy stuff with his car—Mother was always forgetting to buy something, and since she did not drive, Gilles and I frequently had to carry something extra up the hill when we were coming back from school. Often we were bringing home two or three baguettes of still warm crusty French bread. For some reason not one of these baguettes had ends by the time we reached the top of the hill. Coming up from the steps we entered the grounds of Clair Matin through the wooden gate that enchanted Mother the first day she saw it, and walked a hundred feet under an arbor from which in September juicy red and yellow grapes were waiting to be picked.

Our private road, which we had to take care of, was off a public winding street that followed a small narrow valley and which was appropriately named "Le Vallonet." Since 1950 the name Vallonet has become world famous because it was given to a cave discovered by a young girl after a serious mud slide occurred. The cave, which is at the end of the street at the bottom of a 300 foot limestone hill, contains the earliest known working tools (chipped pebbles) of man outside of Africa and the fossil bones of rhinoceroses, elephants, horses and whales, which have been estimated to be 800,000 years old. Our private road led up the hill to the car garage which was built on a terrace at least forty feet higher up than the one on which the house was built. A stoned path edged with cacti, prickly pears and agaves, led down to the house.

The bedroom that Gilles and I shared had a large Roman terrace overhanging a garden in which a large assortment of fruit trees grew: apricots, plums, pears, peaches and cherries. Delicious strawberries were also grown. Around the house three large fig trees dropped to the ground the most juicy and sweet figs that one can taste, because they had ripened under the hot September sun until the last minute. In front of the house a large, palm-shaded, flagstone patio edged by orange and lemon trees became a favorite place to drink tea in the afternoon.

No wonder that our mother fell in love with the place the moment she saw it! And no wonder that we had so many relatives and friends visiting us, especially since the house became very large and hospitable after Father added a wing. It had fifteen rooms, including four bedrooms and two bathrooms. Among our frequent visitors was a brother of Father's, named Fernand, who made him the following proposition: he would buy from him three square feet of land which had to be movable for he wanted to be able to sit in a garden chair following the sun around Clair Matin. Though he loved his brother, Father refused to sell him any part of this heaven on earth.

CHAPTER 6

Our Life Before The War

If you come as its guest, asking of its smile, its wines, its sunlight, its friendship, it will open its heart.

L.R. AND D.C. PEATTIE (LE GAI ROYAUME)

Retirement for Father did not mean that he was going to twiddle his thumbs, counting his money and lying in the sun, drinking wine and eating with relish these good provencal dishes for which the French Riviera is famous. He was still young and needed to remain physically and mentally active. Flower farming seemed to him a nice compromise between his strenuous and competitive work in the glass industry and complete retirement. For him, the farm was to be a business that he would personally run, though the actual farming would be done by others.

For decades carnations had been successfully grown on the sunny dry hills of Roquebrune. As cut flowers they were sent on overnight trains to Paris where they were sold to florists in the early morning hours. It seemed natural for us to continue this tradition. In the town of San Remo, on the other side of the border, Father was fortunate to find an Italian family, appropriately named Profumo (profumo means perfume in Italian), who had grown carnations for years and who was willing to come to Clair Matin to do the same. This family consisted of the two parents and their three children who were in their twenties, one son and two daughters. Neither the parents, nor the children spoke one word of French. So Father and Mother had to learn Italian. Soon, of course, the Profumo children started to speak French, but their parents never did in spite of the fact that they remained in a house on our property until 1945.

Besides carnations and roses we grew early vegetables that we sold to local markets. Among them was the provencal blue-violet artichoke that could be sold as early as March to local restaurants. We also grew tomatoes, lettuce, and other vegetables for our own consumption. We harvested a wide range of fruits, from grapes to strawberries. We made our own jams and marmalades. We also made our own wine which was very ordinary, but good enough for us since we drank very little of it and always watered it down. When we had guests who took wine-tasting and drinking seriously, Father in his opinion had to stoop to purchasing some quality wine, but his choice always brought wise remarks from our friends who teased him on his excellent taste in women, but not in wines.

People who bought carnations in florist shops in Paris, London or New York before World War II had no notion of the tremendous work that carnation growing demanded. This flower, which is native to the Southern part of Europe, has been cultivated there for centuries especially on the terraced hills of the Italian and French Riviera between San Remo and Antibes, east and west of Nice. Carnations were—and still are—grown in the open during the Spring and Summer and were protected in late Fall and Winter, but only at night, with mats to guard against frosts. Farming on these steep terraced hills was very difficult because there was no practical way to use any mechanical equipment, not even the smallest tractor. Everything, therefore, had to be done by hand — plowing, planting, watering, weeding, spraying, and harvesting. Carnations were a demanding crop.

We did not grow the carnations from seeds, but from cuttings which were plucked up from parental plants and rooted in the fall. Each cutting was planted by hand in wetted sand within a cold frame which was covered by glass or by mats. Cuttings were kept moist by a slight watering every day. After a month of loving care and after developing strong roots, the young plants were transplanted to their final location onto the terraces, where it was not out of the ordinary to have more than one hundred thousand carnations growing in rows. Each carnation, after having been planted by hand by someone on his or her knees, was immediately watered with a hose. As soon as the plants had established themselves, it was necessary that they be supported, otherwise they would have fallen over. Therefore stakes, three feet tall and one inch wide were driven into the ground in such a way that each plant was at the center of a four stake square, supported by cotton twine wrapped around the sticks. Additional wrappings were made as the plants grew.

In order to shelter the carnations against the winter cold, in the late fall wooden stakes were driven into the ground along the edges of a block of three plant rows and a frame was made to support straw mats that were religiously rolled down late in the afternoon and rolled up in the early morning hours. In winter very few carnations bloom. This is, of course, the time of the year when people want them. I remember that one day in December Father received a desperate phone call from a florist in Monaco who wanted three dozen white carnations for a wedding. He answered that he did not have any. The florist insisted: "But, Mr. Corcos, we will pay anything for these flowers. Can't you go and see if you have any?" Well, Father went and found six that he delivered. The charge for these six carnations was greater than what thirty dozen of them would have cost in the fall. After all, Father had to unroll and roll back many mats before he found these six solitary white carnations.

Mat rolling, like everything else that has to do with the growing of carnations, was done by hand. But the worse part I remember was the way we controlled the insects and diseases that affect this plant. Twice a week a man had to carry a knapsack pump on his back to dust or spray each plant. Watering was done with a hand hose. How water came to a farm is interesting. County water was piped to big tanks at the bottom of the hill and pumped to large open tanks at the top of our property. Since there was no device to judge the level of water in the upper tanks from the house, the only way to do this was to climb up and see for ourselves. If the water was down someone had to go down the whole hill and start the pumps. The main problem was that the pump could be running, but the water might not, and there was no way of knowing until one had climbed back up to the house to see whether or not the water was spouting out of the pipe on top of the tank. If the water was not running, back down one would go to check the pump. I have often wondered, considering today's high technology, if at that time there could at least have been a way to run a telephone line from the bottom of the hill to the house. This would have saved us numerous trips.

Taking care of a carnation farm in the 1930's was healthy work, but very tough. At least, as children, we did not have to do much of this work. After the war, however, I took over the management of the farm, coming to the obvious conclusion after two years that this type of farming was inefficient to say the least. This is what prompted me to leave France in 1947 in order to study modern horticulture in sunny California, which in many ways reminded me of the beautiful part of France where I was raised.

Father was happy at Clair Matin. He took care of the accounting for the farm business and the transporting of the flowers and vegetables to the railway station, city markets, or the grocery stores. His work schedule left him plenty of time to enjoy many hours of sunshine on the front terrace, smoking his pipe and sharing stories and jokes with friends or relatives. In his big study he loved to listen to recordings of classical music that he played on one of the most modern phonographs of the time. For years he did not have a radio. He did not think he needed one. But his brother, Fernand, thought otherwise. After all, the world was in turmoil and Father should be informed. So one day in 1937, Uncle Fernand, who was at Clair Matin for a few days, asked me for a good-looking envelope and the best writing paper in the house. Then in his superb handwriting he wrote the following:

My dear Brother:

Throw your d.... phonograph through the window and buy yourself the most expensive radio you can find.

Love,

Fernand.

Then he gave me the letter and told me to give it to Father as soon as he had left town, which I did. Father did not throw his phonograph through the window, but he did buy a radio and discovered that for years he had missed listening to the outstanding classical music programs broadcast from Radio Monte Carlo.

Between 1933 and 1939 life was very good to us. But throughout these years France teetered on the brink of civil war. It seems that France is always on the verge of some political upheaval. On the one hand, the rightwing was fearful that the communists would seize power. On the other hand the left wing was afraid that the extreme right would topple the Republic. On the evening of February 6, 1934, I overheard the strangest telephone conversation between Father who was in Paris and Mother who was at home. It went like this:

Father: Well. It was very serious.

Mother. Oh. It was.

Father: Did you hear about it?

Mother: Of course. It was terrible.

Father: There were a lot of casualties.

Mother: No! There were none.

Father: Of course, there were a lot on the bridge.
Mother: What are you talking about the bridge!
Father: The Concorde bridge over the Seine.

It finally dawned on them that they were talking about two different things. Mother was talking about a very violent, windy storm that toppled many trees on our hills. Father was talking about the unsuccessful march of some 40,000 right wing demonstrators on the Assembly. They were stopped by the police on the Concorde bridge over the Seine within a block of the parliament building. It had been a bloody battle for a few hours but the Republic had been saved.

Soon after, reacting to this danger from the right, the left, including the socialists and communists, closed ranks to form a common antifascist front, the popular Front, which two years later swept into power under the leadership of Léon Blum. For Mother, who was and remained a socialist throughout her life, this was her day. We went to the beach that particular afternoon and she shared with her two young boys her hopes for a better society. Mother never joined the socialist party, but she was a socialist at heart because she favored social reforms, such as national health insurance and pre-school nurseries to improve the lives of working men and women. Mother, I say, was a socialist, not a communist. There were tremendous differences between communism and socialism. Contrary to the communist party which was revolutionary and under the orders of the Soviet Union, the socialist party advocated and is still advocating reforms, not revolutions, to get its policies accepted. The break between the French communists and socialists occurred in 1920 at the XVIII National Congress of the Socialist party in the town of Tours. A minority of the members refused to accept the Third International Communist program and split from the majority which became the French communist party with its adherence to Moscow. The Minority kept the name (S.F.I.O.) and became the socialist party, whose leaders were, besides Léon Blum, Jean Longuet and Paul Faure.

With the sweeping of power of the Popular Front in 1936 changes occurred in the leadership of the local government of Roquebrune. Early that year Father had been asked to add his name to a list of people who, dissatisfied with the way the commune was administered, thought they could do a better job. They thought that Father, having been a successful business man, would be an asset in managing the business of the community. After some reflection, he decided to accept the challenge. In France people are not elected on an individual basis, but as members of a political group. To his astonishment, Father found that he and his newly found friends had been elected on a landslide and he was now the vice mayor of the commune. For the first time in his life he was an official in the community in which he lived. Gilles and I were very proud of him, though we did not know exactly what his job consisted of. A few months later, we were told that among his official duties he had the authority to perform marriages. To us children, this was really impressive.

The day after the election, as Father and Mother were sitting on the front terrace, they heard a three man band playing drums, saxophone, and trumpet. The music was not too bad, for some of the tunes were recognizable. Soon the band appeared on the terrace and continued to play for a few minutes. Shortly, Father realized that it was a local tradition for new members of the council to be serenaded. And Mother realized that she had better get some glasses and some wine to celebrate her husband's election. The trumpeter, Mr. Viale, was a character who lived on the top of our hill. He was well known for spending every franc he made on wine. But he knew how to play the trumpet and one of his official jobs was to play the trumpet on the Fourteenth of July, the day that the French people celebrate their liberation from the tyranny of the King. It was on that day, in 1789, that they stormed the Bastille, where the king's enemies were jailed for years without trial.

The mayor of the Commune did not want Mr. Viale to be drunk on that particular day and so every year on the eve of Bastille Day he had him put in jail. The next day, a sober Mr. Viale would play the trumpet and patriotic speeches would be made in the Place des Frères square in Roquebrune village. All kinds of toasts would be given. One particular Bastille day—it must have been in 1937—, as every one was listening with great attention to an important official speech, Mother happened to have her eyes on the zinc table next to her, where she had left her half-full wine glass. She saw a little hand removing the glass of wine. Looking under the table, she discovered a boy of nine years quietly drinking her wine, smacking his lips. Mother found this very funny. In any event, since French kids are not forbidden to drink wine, there was little she could have done even if she had wanted to.

Father remained an official of the commune for ten years. However, not only Father, but Mother also played an important role in the community.

Mother established a dispensary to take care of the health of the numerous underpriviledged children of Roquebrune. She had a Master's degree in Biology from the University of Paris and a diploma in nursing from the Red Cross. The health of children was a primary concern for her and in a sense she had missed a vocation for which she would have been well-suited— that of a pediatrician. However, she did not go on to become a physician. Instead, after meeting her "charming prince" in 1914, she married him two weeks before World War I began when she was twenty-two and he thirty. At the end of World War I she became his business partner, abandoning any thoughts of going to medical school.

However, she never forgot her dream of being involved in some way in the field of medicine and the opportunity to do so came in 1936. When we were still in grammar school, Mother realized that the children around us lacked medical care. Though these children were checked twice a year by a county physician, there was no attempt by the county to see that his recommendations were followed. The parents of most of the children were illiterate farm laborers who had emigrated from Italy. Being very poor, they could not afford to see a physician or a dentist. Mother thought that she might be able to do something to improve the health of the children of the community. She had in mind the establishment of a dispensary, similar to one she had known in Paris, the aim of which was preventive medicine for children of school age. Medical inspection was followed by home visits made by social workers or nurses who helped the children's parents correct any health problems that had been detected.

At first Mother's dispensary at Roquebrune ran into the ordinary problems that any new establishment of that sort would encounter: lack of funds and very little support from the community. But Mother got immediate help from Father who happened to be, as vice-mayor of Roquebrune, responsible for medical affairs in the commune. He was able to find an empty unutilized room in the County Hall where the dispensary could be located. The County employees seemed to have been more interested in what Mother was trying to accomplish than the local politicians who, like politicians from any place, were more interested in their reelection than in the health of children. The carpenter offered to make furniture for the office and the examination room. Other employees offered their time to clean up and paint the place. Mother then looked for a physician. This was not easy, for most of them thought that a free clinic would cut down their profits. Finally she found one who was willing to help with very little monetary reward. According to Mother he was an excellent diagnostician, but had no bedside manners whatsoever, although he did have a caustic sense of humor. This did not bother Mother who helped him by taking care of all the records. They became good friends and remained friends for years.

The next member of the team that Mother had to get was the visiting nurse. Mother did not look for her, for she practically dropped out of the sky. One day Mother received a phone call from a woman, named Bouverot who, with her husband, a Physical Education High School Instructor, had just moved to Menton. Madame Bouverot, a social worker with a nursing degree, proposed to Mother to work with her, first on a voluntary basis, then later when the dispensary was hopefully funded, she would be paid accordingly. Mother accepted and soon found out that Madame Bouverot was a superb social worker who was always willing to see the children's parents and talk to them. These home visits were not easy to make since most of the houses she went to had to be reached by foot, climbing up and down steep hills.

To make the story short, Mother's dispensary was a total success. She was able to convince many physicians and dentists to give free consultations because they finally realized that they were gaining future patients who, as children, had taken the habit of being regularly checked by a physician and a dentist. Mother soon was able to fund the dispensary. Father's friends on the council, realizing that it was politically helpful after all to have the County associated with the welfare of the children, gave a grant. Later the Health Department of the Alpes Maritimes also contributed money. Finally the Ministry of Health decided to support the programs financially. Besides these public funds Mother was able to get private donations from the many British and American citizens who owned beautiful villas in the community, one of which belonged to Winston Churchill where he passed many days painting in his garden.

Father and Mother were happy. Their life was meaningful, for they had found a beautiful place to be and work and now they were helping the community. They had excellent friends. Among them was a famous painter, whom everyone, including his wife, called Vanden (his real name was far too long for anyone to remember). He used to come often from his house in the old village of Roquebrune through the hills to our house to paint flowers in our garden (he was particularly fond of roses). Once he painted Mother. Gilles and I still have that painting, as well as others that he either gave or sold to our parents. As Vanden was an excellent conversationalist, our parents enjoyed having him for lunch or for tea. He knew how to tell stories. The one that always impressed me was the following:

Many years ago there was an old Arab who had three sons. He died leaving a will in which he left half his estate to his eldest son; one third to his second son, and one ninth to his third son. His estate consisted of seventeen mules. As soon as he left this earth, his three sons started fighting. His eldest son wanted 9 mules, which was more than his share. His second son wanted six mules, which also was more than his share. His youngest son wanted two mules, which also was more than his share. After finding out that it was very hard to divide 17 mules according to their father's wish, they called on a cadi (a judge) to solve this touchy problem. The cadi thought for a while (the reader can do the same). After half an hour he called to his attendant: "Mohamed, go to the barn and get my mule." As soon as the mule was there, he started to distribute the estate. He gave 9 mules to the eldest son, six mules to the second son, and two mules to the third. Then, he said: "Mohamed, bring back my mule to the stable."

I used this story a few times to teach high school students that Mathematics has drawbacks- fractions of an odd number such as 17 never total a whole unit. My students were very impressed for no one before had ever illustrated to them the nature of mathematics with stories.

Our parents were happy for another reason as well. They had two nice, handsome and healthy boys whose main duty was to go to school. When Gilles and I were children, education was compulsory for all until the age of fourteen, emphasizing the elements of general culture and, optionally, the rudiments of professional and technical training. Education was not only obligatory and free but identical. As this implies, a child, provided he or she has the qualifications, should receive the same education, whether in the heart of Paris or in an isolated valley of Auvergne; in a high school in the Latin Quarter or in a rural town. But, in fact, this was not always so. A child raised in a large city had a better chance to get a good education than one raised in a small town. And unfortunately this happened to Gilles and me.

For the first two years, we went to the local public grammar school. However, it became obvious to our parents that we were not getting much of an education there and they transferred us to a private Catholic school where the instruction was better. Though we were not supposed to get any religious schooling, as Father, a strong anticlerical, had asked, we did get some. I'm completely sure it did not hurt us. In France there are private schools. However, in order to graduate from them, their students like those of public schools have to pass national exams. Performance on these exams is judged by teachers who do not know the identity of the students.

In 1936, at the age of eleven I had finished grammar school. If I were to continue my education I had to go to the local high school at Menton. There is no such thing as junior high school in France. Entry to high school which covers six grades was by examination. Not every one then would be going to high school. Many children went to trade schools. Who went to high school and who went to trade school was not necessarily determined by the grades or scores he or she got at school, but more by family tradition and pressure. Though one could find in high schools quite a few academic, highly successful and highly motivated children from lower classes, most of the students were from middle and upper classes.

That Gilles and I would go to high school had been decided by our parents a long time before we went. I successfully passed the entrance exam and in the fall of 1936 every day of the week, except Thursday and Sunday -there are no classes on those days-, I rode my bicycle to the high school for boys which was two miles away from home. The high school for girls was in another part of town. French people are firm believers in the separation of sexes between ten and 18 years of age. Maybe they know something that Americans do not know.

I stayed on the school grounds for lunch eating sandwiches. Very rarely did I buy a piece of pissaladiere from the janitor's wife. Pissaladiere has become very popular in the States under the name of pizza. But let's face it. The original made on the French or Italian Riviera is far better than the U.S. facsimile, not so much because of its contents, but because of its dough which reminds any real connoisseur of real French bread.

I do not remember much of what I did this first year in high school, except that some students drove some of our teachers crazy by putting from time to time incendiary material in inkpots. A fire would start immediately and had to be extinguished before it spread to the old wooden tables. I remember well one of my teachers who taught us science, mostly biology. He had lost his right arm during World War I and wrote on the blackboard with his left hand with his empty right sleeve in his coat pocket. But what impressed me more than his physical disability was his wisdom. He gave me something to think about democracy by stressing a drawback of universal voting. He said to the class: "Suppose that you people find a snake, but cannot agree whether it is or not a viper. You decide to settle the question by a vote. The results are the following: 19 of you say it is not a viper. Only one of you says it is. By majority vote the snake is therefore claimed not to be a viper. But it happens that the only one of you who voted the snake to be a viper is the son of a man who is an expert in snake recognition. Having been well taught by his father he is able to recognize a viper when he sees it." I think that the teacher's point was that voting is not always the way to solve a problem, certainly not a scientific one. I could agree with that, but did he also want to tell us that no one should be allowed to vote on any issue unless one is an expert in the field related to that issue? I never knew the answer to this question. Being too young and shy I never dared to ask my teacher what he really thought about democracy and the right to vote. I have since realized that most citizens vote on issues without really having made any study of them. But I still firmly believed that, with all its drawbacks, democracy, and with it the universal right to vote, is the best type of government.

That first year in high school I had to take up one or two foreign languages. Though Mother spoke German and could have helped me in that language, my parents decided I should learn English. That was a wise decision for it is now spoken all over the world. They also decided that I should learn Latin. That was a bad decision. They had been influenced by a cousin of theirs who happened to be a Latin teacher in Monaco and who believed, like other Latin teachers, that in order to master French one should know its linguistic roots. Though I was rather good in Latin and had six years of it, I never was convinced that it helped me in any way in reading or writing my native language. I think I would have made better use of my time by learning Italian or German. The following year Gilles entered high school and I was not alone any more riding my bicycle back and forth to Menton.

One thing I remember is that we had a lot of homework to do in every field, be it history, French literature, mathematics or science. Father, who never went to high school helped us in French. I do not know why he and his brothers were so literate in French, but all of them were. They could write beautifully. Mother helped us with biology and mathematics. As we progressed in school, however, we were left more and more on our own. But by then we had the background and the appreciation necessary to continue our studies as far as we wanted to, which we did.

Our school work left us plenty of time to play around Clair Matin, climbing trees, running up and down the hill, doing all the crazy things that boys do, including fighting with the neighbor kids with slingshots until one of us was hurt, though not seriously. We did a lot of gymnastics on a big gym set that Father had had built next to the house. As early as April we went with Mother to the beach and swam in the sea. The local people, who generally waited until late June to swim, thought we were crazy to do it so early in the season, but not as crazy as the English who started in March. Father, who did not like to swim, used to join us later on the beach and gave us a car ride back home. Another of our favorite sports was skiing which we did in the French or Swiss Alps. More about our love of skiing later.

We liked to play soccer with the kids in the neighborhood on the communal "soccer" stadium which was below our hill. The French call soccer "football." They are right. The Americans are wrong. After all, soccer is played with the foot, not with the hand, so American football should be called something else. Soccer is very important in the life of the French, old and young. There were important games played on that soccer field, such as the team of Menton against the sailors of a British ship anchored in the Bay. One particular Sunday Gilles and I, wanting to see one of these "international games," climbed over the wall instead of coming through the gate as decent citizens should. We were caught by the local cop who said to us: "Are you not the Corcos children? Why on earth do you climb over the wall when your father, the vice-mayor, can get free passes to see any soccer game?" Father had never told us that. Neither he nor Mother had ever been soccer fans and never thought that their children could be.

Sometimes on Sunday afternoons Gilles and I joined Father and other men in playing a game of Pétanque. This is the game that the Italians and the Americans called Bocce and that the French who live outside the Provence call boules. Each player has two or three heavy steel balls, or boules, identified by different patterns etched into the steel, one in each hand, that make a happy clack when tapped together. The objective of the game is to throw the boules as close as possible to a very small wooden ball, called le cochonnet or little pig, that is tossed up the court. At the end of the round the closest to the cochonnet is the winner. If the boule of your adversary is so close to the cochonnet that it is impossible for you to come closer, you are expected to knock away the ball of your adversary by hitting it with your own boule by rolling it on the ground or by throwing it. On the Riviera la pétanque is the local past time of the French, who are known to play the game everywhere, in all public squares and side streets of the provincial towns. Streetcars have been known to stop in order for games to continue uninterrupted.

At Clair Matin, Father had converted part of a terrace into a pétanque court. The ground was regularly rolled with a big and heavy hand-pulled cement roller. One day, Gilles and I and two other kids who were all around ten years of age started moving this roller just for fun. Of course, we had been warned not to do so and for good reason. We soon found out that we could not control the roller which weighted more than 200 pounds. It left off the smooth court and began rolling down the edge of the terrace, fell to the second terrace, the third, the fourth, and finally hit a large olive tree at the bottom of the hill. It was obvious that we had to tell Father about this childish and irresponsible thing that we had done. The roller did not hurt anyone or anything, but it could have. After seriously chiding us, Father talked to Senior Profumo who asked his son, Roberto to get the roller at the bottom of the hill. Roberto was then 20 years old, handsome as a Greek god, especially when he was tanned, and as strong as an ox. He picked up the roller, put it on one of his shoulders and slowly climbed up the hill one terrace after the other. Gilles and I were impressed and never touched the roller again.

A few years later, a long-time friend of my parents, called Fernand Rocoffort, bought the flower farm next door to us. He joined the pétanque team and on a Sunday afternoon, as he was playing, a man who was the local rebouteux, a non-licensed chiropractor, asked him why he was limping. Mr. Rocoffort told him that during a skiing trip, he had broken his ankle which had been set by a famous surgeon in Paris and since then he had been limping. The rebouteux told him to sit on a chair, and without asking his permission, he pulled Rocoffort's foot, twisting the ankle until he heard the special noise of a bone snapping in place. Monsieur Rocoffort yelled like a pig in a slaughterhouse, but to his stupefaction he discovered that his ankle did not hurt anymore and an hour later he could walk like an ordinary human being. Welcome to the unsophisticated medicine of the French Riviera.

Gilles and I lived eight happy years of our childhood on the French Riviera. Though we were both born in Paris we acted like the children around us and to the dismay of Mother, who was born and raised in Paris, we even talked like them. We had the Southern accent, which God knows is so different from the "sophisticated" Parisian accent. We used local expressions unknown to people outside La Provence. Mother did not blame this on the fact that we were raised in the region, but on the fact that we often repeated word for word, with the accent of Provence, the everlasting films of Marcel Pagnol, Marius, Fanny and Cesar. These told, in the vernacular and with wit, the story of three generations of a family from Marseilles. Personally, I never had the problem so common to the new generation of trying to answer the question, who am I? I always knew who I was. I am a child of Provence and I still have my Southern accent.

We were leading "the life of Riley." Would it end? Unfortunately it did in the Spring of 1940.

PART 4

THE ROAD TO HELL

CHAPTER 7

The War And Us

The French flag is taken down...

During the phoney war life around us went on as usual. Though there were French troops in the forts above our house and in the barracks at the bottom of our hills, the war seemed far away. Gilles and I, like many other French children, had to continue our education. So, every school morning we walked down the 99 steps to the bottom of the hill, picked up our bicycles in one shed of a retired warrant officer, bicycled to the high school which was located in the center of Menton. And in the afternoon we cycled back, leaving our bicycles in the shed, and climbed once more the 99 steps up the hill. Twice a month on Friday afternoon the warrant officer received his pension money and immediately spent most of it drinking. On these Friday afternoons we always found him asleep on a chair in his garden, and is wife sitting on one of the 99 steps up the hill because she was afraid to stay home and be beaten. The reason we left our bicycles at the bottom of the hill was because of the steepness of the road that led to our house. It was easier and faster to walk up the hill. Of course it would have been faster to ride down the hill, but within a week we would not have had any more brakes.

The winter came. It was a harsh one. One evening it snowed—a rare event. During the night we helped Father who was trying to prevent frost damage to the carnations, roses and calla lilies in the greenhouses by lighting up kerosene stoves. The snow melted the next morning, but there was some serious damage to the outside water pipes which were not buried in the ground. Spring came, but with it came the onslaught of the German Army, and soon the fall of Paris.

On June 10 Benito Mussolini chose to declare war on France. It was on this day that his troops crossed the border hoping to penetrate far into France, at least as far as Nice, a part of the Riviera that he had coveted for many years. But his dream was not to be realized. Though the French troops were demoralized knowing that the war was lost, they decided to teach the Italians a lesson for having plunged a knife in their country's back. Well situated in their mountain fortresses of Mont Agel and Tête des Chiens they used heavy artillery to repulse the Italian assault.

We did not witness this battle in which thousands of Italian soldiers were killed. By then we and all our neighbors had left our homes. When the Germans started their offensive in May, the French High Command ordered all the inhabitants of Menton and Roquebrune to leave the region, because, being on the edge of Italy, it had become a potential war zone.

We were told we could move into the town of Antibes thirty miles westward on the French Riviera. Antibes, being a tourist town, had at that time many unoccupied houses and it was possible to find lodging there. So, like our neighbors we left everything behind us and hit the road. We were sad of course to leave our cherished home, but we hoped that this uprooting was a temporary one. We were mistaken. Neither we nor any the other member of the community came back for four long years, because in June of 1940 Italy annexed Menton and its immediate surroundings as a self-reward for having entered the war on the side of Hitler at the last minute. Menton remained in Italian hands until the Japanese-American forces liberated it from the German occupation in 1944.

Our parents decided not to go to Antibes right away, but to go to Paris by car and see the rest of the family. This was a big mistake. We never reached Paris. Instead we got caught in an exodus of refugees which, like a big unfurling ocean wave, blocked our passage and forced us to go back where we came from.

In the Summer of 1940, like all French citizens, we were stunned by the defeat of our country. Being young at the time, I did not have much of an idea of why such a catastrophe had occurred. However, I heard around me that neither France nor England had been military ready when they declared war on Germany. According to Father, always critical of the military, the French generals, who by now had thoroughly understood how they should have won World War I, had no idea how they should have won World War II. They were always one war behind. Unfortunately for us, Father had been right. As late as 1939, the French High Command seemed to have no notion of modern warfare (1940 style) which was fought with tanks, planes, and parachutists. The French Army which should have had a large number of anti-tanks and anti-aircraft guns, had very few of these. It was reported that even officers did not have enough revolvers. During the eight months of the phoney war the French did not do much to catch up with the Germans. In fact, the workers who knew how to build tanks and planes had been mobilized and were busy peeling potatoes and cleaning floors instead of working overtime in armament factories. French experts were sure that by 1942 there would be enough tanks and planes to smash the third Reich. But they had no idea that the Germans would win the war by 1940. They were under the impression that modern wars last at least four years. Of course, the French could have bought the modern equipment that they needed from the Americans, but they did not do this on a large scale for two reasons. The economists thought it wiser to keep dollars and gold in France and the industrialists lobbied against buying material from foreigners.

However, the lack of military material could not be blamed entirely on the generals who did not ask for it. The blame must be shared also by the politicians of the left who thought that if the army became too strong the generals would take over the Republic, just as General Bonaparte did in the 18th century and General Boulanger in the nineteenth century. This fear was also real among the French people, including Mother who was telling me in 1947, two years after the end of the war, that we should not give too much constitutional power to the President of the Republic because she feared that if de Gaulle, being a general, were elected President sooner or later he would become a dictator.

Another view that I heard was that we had enough arms, but because of negligence or ill will there had been a failure to get all the arms and ammunition out the arsenals and depots into the hands of the soldiers on the front. As evidence, it was reported that when the Germans occupied France they found enormous unused supplies of weapons.

Whatever the true reason is for the military defeat of France there is no doubt that internal politics played a great role in that defeat. I heard around me that France had been defeated not by the mighty Wermacht, but by treason on the part of a large number of Frenchmen, including military officers, who preferred fascism to democracy and who had delivered their country to their partisans beyond the Rhine. It was well known that even before the war there had been collaboration between the Nazis and some Frenchmen who, as members of what has been called the Fifth Column, prepared the conquest of France by Germany by spying on French citizens and demoralizing them. Our own family was directly affected by a fifth column member who, for a few years, had been the chauffeur of one of my uncles. After the collapse of France, the former chauffeur returned to Paris as a Nazi officer and shot my uncle in cold blood, most likely because having been fired, he hated him.

After the fall of Paris Father plainly saw that nothing would stop the German forces. He did not need to be a prophet to realize that the future of France was very dark. Furthermore he feared that staying in France under the Germans was to put his family in danger. Again he thought of the Nazi definition of a Jew. Though we did not practice in any way the Jewish faith, the fact that we had some ancestors two or three generations back who did put us on the list of the undesirables. Though Father could not predict the extent of the holocaust, he rightly sensed that it was better for us to leave Metropolitan France. The future of our country, he thought, was now in the hands of the English and possibly soon in the hands of the Americans. Hoping that he could help the Allied cause overseas, he decided that we should go to England. We needed to reach a harbor. Bordeaux on the Atlantic coast seemed to be the best choice because we had heard that the French Government had considered going from Bordeaux to Algiers to continue the fight there. So, we attempted to go to Bordeaux by car hoping to find passage there to North Africa or to England. But we never reached our destination.

On our way to Bordeaux, we again got caught in the traffic of hundred of thousands of people who, like us, were attempting to reach the Atlantic coast. Many people we saw looked sick and miserable, ragged and obviously in need of the simplest essentials, such as potable water and edible food. There were not only civilians, but numerous retreating distraught soldiers who did not know where to go or what to do. Many of these soldiers had taken off their shoes, exposing their bloody feet injured by long marches. Some of them had replaced part of their uniforms with civilian clothes, such as overcoats, hats, and scarves.

On our way we stopped at a family friend's home at Figeac in Central France where we heard worse news. France through the intermediary of Pétain, was asking for an armistice. I still remember a wise old farmer on the side of the road who told us his interpretation of the establishment of Pétain as the chief of Government. —"If they replace Pétain by one of his statues, it will have the same effect on Hitler."

Personally, I never understood what the Old Marshal meant by "making the gift" of his person. After all, he was not going to jail or in front of a firing squad. He had become the head of the French Government. Such a position did not look to me to be a bad job. I did not pay much attention to Pétain at the time. I was far more interested in de Gaulle whose position was far clearer to me than the one of Pétain.

I did not hear De Gaulle's message, but knew about it. I can truly say that I was a Gaullist from day one. If I had been two years older I might have tried to join de Gaulle in England on my own, for many 17 year olds did.

I met one of these audacious teenagers two months after the war was over. He had gone to England in July 1940 canoeing across the Channel. You have to be crazy or be a 17 year old to attempt to do this. Well, he succeeded. He did not join de Gaulle, but the Royal Air Force. Five years later when I saw him at the ministry of Air in Paris he was a captain and he wanted to be discharged. The sergeant in charge of the rubber stamp was telling him it was impossible for him to be discharged by the French Air Force since he never belonged to it. But the Captain insisted, after all he was French and not English and he was sure that he would be drafted by the French if there was no record that he served in the Armed Forces. So, the exasperated sergeant used his official rubber stamp and the Captain was discharged from the British Air Force by the French Government.

The Captain had guessed right, for three months later we were all to report for the draft as any twenty one year old should. But the French Government discovered that 75 percent of us had already served in some capacity either in the regular armed forces, Allied or French, in the forces of the interior (FFI), or even labor camps. So in its wisdom it decided that all the young men born in the years 1920 through 1925 were declared to be in the reserves.

The Wermacht reached Bordeaux before we ever did. It seemed that the door to freedom was now closed. Were we going to be prisoners in France at the mercy of the Nazis? We thought that there might still be hope. It was obvious that the only harbors from which we could take a boat to go to England now were those on the Mediterranean coast. So we went as fast as possible to Port Vendres at the Spanish border. There was a lonely English boat ready to leave either during the night or early morning. Father was told that the Captain might accept a few passengers just a few minutes before departure. Very tired, we decided to sleep a few hours in a hotel. However, before retiring in our rooms, Father bribed an English sailor to tell him when the boat was leaving for sure. But the boat left just as we got up the next morning. We suspected that the Captain was more interested in taking aboard young men ready to fight than us. After all, Father was too old and Gilles and I were too young. To our chagrin we saw the boat disappearing over the southern horizon. This was the last English boat we saw for four years. We felt that the last door to freedom had been slammed in our faces. That day the Vichy Government prevented anyone from leaving France without its approval. All borders were closed. Spain under Franco was an ally of Hitler and we did not attempt to cross its border. We felt betrayed by "our own government." We could accept the crush of our country by the mighty German forces, but we could not accept that a French government could prevent its citizens to continue the fight against an enemy ready to destroy all of what our country stood for. All of a sudden the terms liberty, equality and fraternity, were not just words inscribed on flags, words that politicians use only on the 14th of July or in their reelection campaigns, but real concepts that were on the verge of disappearing from our lives. Our parents realized this, but they could not imagine how far the Vichy Government would collaborate with the Nazis.

Chapter 8

Return To The French Riviera

Between the white meerschaum at the foot of the walls and the white snow at the edge of the sky, the small shinning city standing in front of the blue background of the first mountains offered to the rays of a setting sun a pyramid of red roofed houses, whose fronts were also white, but so different that they seemed to be of all colors.

GUY DE MAUPASSANT WRITING ABOUT ANTIBES

Having missed the last boat to England, our heartbroken parents decided to leave Port Vendres and go back to the French Riviera. We stopped at Antibes, a town of twenty thousand people, thirteen miles west of Nice. Many inhabitants of Menton and Roquebrune had moved to Antibes after having left their homes when the war broke out with Italy. Now, like us, they could not go back because in June of 1940 their land had been annexed by the Italians. We looked for a home in Antibes and we rented a house for a few weeks until Father could find something to do, possibly managing another flower farm. After all, Antibes, like Menton, was well-known for its commercial production of roses and carnations. The main market was Paris which had come a long way since the famous journalist Alphonse Karr had written about the opportunities the newly built railway offered for shipping cut flowers to the French Capital.

The region of Antibes is similar to many parts of Greece, and it is possible that for this reason the Greeks of Marseilles felt so at home there that in the fourth century they founded a town that they called Antipolis. Five hundred years later, Antipolis fell under the influence of the Romans who built a circus, a theater, baths and aqueducts which remained more or less intact until Vauban, the famous French 17th century engineer, helped himself generously to the stones of these ancient monuments to build fortifications around the town, leaving only ruins of these Roman buildings. However, because of these solid fortifications, the town, now called Antibes, was able to successfully defend itself against attacks of various enemies and had remained French ever since. At the end of the nineteenth century these fortifications were removed and a new part of the town was built on their site.

The coastal region of Antibes reminded us of that of Menton. There is a peninsula, the Cap d'Antibes, which separates two very different communities, Juan Les Pins on the western side and Antibes proper on the eastern side. Like the Cap Martin at Roquebrune, the Cap d'Antibes, is surmounted by a lighthouse and has luxurious residences and hotels nestled among pines. The coast from Juan Les Pins to the end of the cape is exquisite, with little creeks and bays with sandy beaches, but the coast on the eastern side from the Cape to the harbor of Antibes is untidy. Juan Les Pins, the touristic part of Antibes, has really only come into existence since 1928. It was then that foreigners discovered its long sandy beach and since then have invaded the town, launching the summer season and making its fortune in tourism. Before the war Antibes was the rendez-vous of would-be famous artists and writers. Claude Monet and Guy de Maupassant were enraptured by the beauty of the region. It was in Antibes that Jules Verne wrote Twenty Thousands Leagues Under The Sea and Graham Greene, Chagrin in Three Parts. It was also here that Corot painted some of his masterpieces.

The house that we rented on a monthly basis was at the edge of Juan Les Pins and Antibes, a few hundred feet from a foot path that goes around the Cap d'Antibes. My parents loved to take walks and they soon discovered that the one around the Cape was delightful. One Sunday afternoon as the four of us were strolling on the path, we passed a couple with their three children whom Gilles and I immediately recognized as schoolmates of ours back in Menton. Their father was a physician, Dr. Pouget, a well-known right winger, whose political views opposed those of our parents. We had gone only a few hundred yards when the physician and his family turned back and hurried to talk to us. Dr. Pouget said that his children had told him who we were and he wanted our parents to know that, though they were politically at the antipodes of each other, he was a patriot and wanted the Germans out of our country. He added that he would do anything to that end. He asked us if he could help us in any way. Our father thought that Dr. Pouget was sincere and both men shook hands. Later Dr. Pouget became our family physician. We discovered that patriotism was not the virtue of one particular political group, but could be found among people who otherwise had nothing in common. In the light of common danger such as Hitlerism they would unite. This was to happen time and time again during the German occupation of France.

A few days later Uncle Fernand -the same uncle who told Father to throw his phonograph through the window- and his wife, Alice, came to visit us before they left for Mexico. How they were able to go to Mexico when it was legally forbidden to leave France makes a curious human story. Uncle Fernand was going on an official state mission. How did he get such an honor?

Uncle Fernand was a well-known lawyer who loved to defend honest but poor people. He could afford to do this because his wife had money. He was very much active in politics —many lawyers seem to be, whether they are French or American. He had run unsuccessfully for a senate seat a few years before. I suspect that the reason for his failure was that he was too honest: he could not lie, a real drawback when trying to win an election. He was a liberal and was proud to have been for many years the secretary of la Ligue des Droits de l'Homme (National League of Human Rights). He was an important member in the Radical Socialist party which, according to him, was a mix of very honest people and great

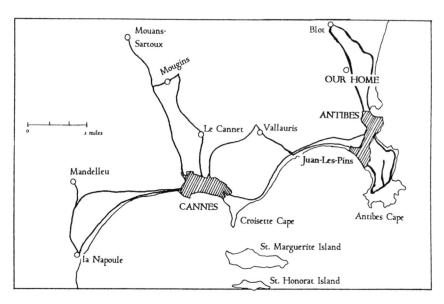

Antibes and its surroundings

crooks. Among the crooks was Pierre Laval who was at that time the Vice-Prime Minister in the Vichy Government and who came to be the epitome of the collaborator. Eventually he was shot as a traitor a few months after the liberation of France. However, before the war, Laval and Uncle Fernand were excellent friends. They often ate at each other's homes and discussed endlessly and vehemently, as only two Frenchmen can do, the political future of their country. Their friendship paid off for my uncle. Though in 1940, they were now politically at the antipodes of each other, Laval realized that if my uncle, a well-known anti-nazi, were to stay in France, sooner or later he would be caught by the Gestapo and shot. He did not want this to happen so he sent my uncle on an official mission to Mexico, knowing perfectly well that he would not be back. It is hard to understand how a man like Laval, who later helped the Germans by sending thousands of Frenchmen to work as slaves in war factories, rounded up thousands of Jews, and tracked down thousands of Resistants, decided to save my uncle's life by sending him abroad. But he did.

Uncle Fernand and Aunt Alice stayed with us for a few days. The two brothers had long discussions about the future of France which seemed very bleak indeed. During one of them Uncle Fernand asked an interesting question concerning Gilles and me. Could he take us with him to Mexico? He looked up his diplomatic passport and papers and thought, but was not sure, that he could add his nephews as members of his family. However, for some reason that I have now forgotten, the matter was not pursued and Gilles and I remained with our parents in Antibes, while Uncle Fernand and Aunt Alice left for Mexico through Spain and Portugal.

From there they went directly to New York where they stayed until 1947, far away from their beautiful Parisian apartment, 27 Avenue Foch, within a stone's throw of the headquarters of the Gestapo with its torture chambers. Their own apartment was occupied by German officers throughout the 1940-44 years. It was stripped of all its contents including works of art and books. However, at the end of the war, most of them were unexpectedly found still intact in boxes in a railway car inside Poland, and were sent back to Paris where they found their way into Uncle Fernand and Aunt Alice's apartment.

A month later our parents found a flower farm for sale. They talked the owner into renting it with the understanding that if they were satisfied they would buy it, which they did a year later. But this time we were going to grow roses in greenhouses for the Paris market instead of carnations as we had done at Clair Matin.

The man who sold us the farm was a real character. His name was Tourdre. He was a small, wiry man with a Hitler-like mustache, who dressed badly and who could not read or write. Yet, rumor had it that he was a millionaire. This is not all that surprising, for knowing how to read and write is, of course, helpful in business, but not necessary. Tourdre could always find someone to read his corespondence and contracts to him. Having original ideas can be far more important than being literate, and Tourdre could think. He reminded me of a character in one of Somerset Maugham's short stories. Since Maugham lived for many years in Antibes I wondered whether he had known Mr. Tourdre.

In the short story, "the Verger", Somerset Maughan tells about a fifty year old Church janitor, Albert Edward Foreman, who is fired from his job because he, like Mr. Tourdre, does not know how to read and write. Let go with a month's salary, the janitor walks down the street looking for cigarets. He has to go three miles before he gets some in a tobacco shop. Having a few hundred pounds in the bank he decides to open a tobacco shop close to the Church. In spite of the fact that he still does not know how to read and write his shop prospers and he soon opens up another one. He marries his landlady and becomes a father. He decides to have his little boy baptized at the same church where he had worked as a janitor. When the baptism is over, he leaves fifty pounds in the dish for offerings. The pastor then remarks to him that he must be doing well and asks him to what he attributes his success. The answer comes straightforwardly: "To the fact that I do not know how to read or write, for if I did know, I would still be a janitor in your Church."

Father and Mr. Tourdre hit it off marvelously well, possibly because both had a very keen sense for business matters. I can still see them discussing some important part of a contract. Father had raised the possibility that one of them might die. Mr. Tourdre putting his index finger on his nose as he usually did when arguing, commented with words borrowed from the provincial dialect; that if anyone died, it would not be "cocagne," a very colorful word for "funny."

We moved into one of the two houses on that farm. At least thirty very skinny pigeons nested on the patio of this house. Obviously they had not been fed for a long time and they had not found much food around. Food for us was already scarce and soon the fate of the pigeons was sealed. Though their meat was not exactly tender, we ate them. Eating very skinny pigeons is not representative of French cooking. But these were abnormal times and not only skinny pigeons, but many types of animals, like cats and dogs, that were not generally eaten, disappeared into people's cooking pots.

At the end of the summer of 1940 Gilles and I started another school year at the Collège d'Antibes (the local high school). The school was overcrowded because many children and teachers had transferred from Menton to Antibes. The teaching was very poor. Among the transferred teachers was one who taught chemistry and had a terrible time dividing simple numbers such as 27 by 3. There were two English teachers at this high school as well. The one I had knew enough English to teach it at the high school level, but the one Gilles had was very incompetent. One day he decided to correct my brother's rather good English accent. The word was business. Gilles pronounced it correctly biz'nis. The teacher told him that there were three syllables in this word and its "correct" pronunciation was BU-SI-NESS. What my brother answered, in his beard if he had had one, was that the BUS was not in the word "business", but should be attached to that particular English teacher. It is of course impossible to translate a pun from one language to another. But the French word "buse" means stupid.

There was also a Math teacher who knew mathematics well but was a terror among the students. His name was Mathieu. He had no patience. On the days he felt good he would randomly call up the names of three students who would immediately stand next to the blackboard. Mr. Mathieu would ask them some questions which the poor souls could never answer because either they did not know the answer or they were so scared that they became mute. A few minutes later they were back at their seats having heard that they were beyond any hope. It was obvious according to the teacher, that they should go and milk cows instead of wasting their time trying to be high school graduates. Mr. Mathieu would then call another set of three students, repeating the same questions, and getting no better answer. He would then send the second set of students back to their seats with the same speech he made to the first set of three. The lesson for the day always ended the same way. Mr. Mathieu knew he had only three students who understood mathematics. He called on them and seemed to feel better since they were generally able to answer the questions he asked. I was never in trouble with Mr.Mathieu because I was fortunate enough to be one of the three members of the last group. One day I saw him walking in his small garden at home inspecting his vegetables and I asked him if he was looking for square roots? He did not laugh. It was apparent to me that besides being an impatient and uncompassionate man he had no sense of humor.

The Vichy government brought a slight change in the political environment in our high school. Pictures of Marshal Pétain were conspicuously hung on the walls. The Rooster, the symbol of the French Republic, was replaced by the Francisque, the symbol of l'Etat Français de Monsieur Le Marechal Pétain. The words, LIBERTY, EQUALITY, FRATERNITY had been replaced by the words WORK, FAMILY, and FATHERLAND, which were supposed to call to mind the idea of a peaceful farmer on his land.

We paid little attention to all of this, but something new in the curriculum caught our interest: an emphasis on physical training, particularly in the form of gymnastics. Authoritarian and totalitarian regimes have always attempted to influence youth in this fashion. This was one of the few new things that Gilles and I could accept. We welcomed our new gym classes. The physical education instructor, Monsieur Michel, was the brother in law of one of Gilles best friends, Gilbert Gout. With Gilbert and other schoolmates we joined the local Basketball Club. In France, cities or communes, not schools, have sports teams.

Another change that affected us was the fact that the Vichy Government considered Freemasons its enemies and as early as 1940 kicked them out of the field of education. At least one of our high school teachers who was a freemason lost his job. Father, thinking that he could help him, decided that Gilles and I needed private French lessons. So we went to this teacher's house and learned about French poetry, in particular about the poet Paul Valery. The persecution of the Freemasons by the Vichy Government never had the vicious character it did towards the Jews, but it did paint the reactionary nature of the Vichy Government and its absurdity, because in many cases the removal of excellent civil servants disorganized numerous government civil administrations

CHAPTER 9

Vichy, The Jews And Us

In conclusion we found no difficulty with the Vichy Government in imple-menting Jewish policy.

HELMUT KNODEN. 1947

Before the signing of the Armistice, Father had already predicted that, if France lost the war, Hitler would make life miserable for its citizens and especially for the Jews. What he had not predicted was that the Vichy Government would so willingly take such an active part in the elimination of the Jews.

My parents refused to have anything to do with the Vichy antisemitic decrees. They were completely aware that if they indicated on any official paper that they had any Jewish ancestors, they would be writing not only their own death sentence, but also their children's as well. The establish-ment of a census in October 1940 meant that French citizens had to have a record of their family history. Father dug up appropriate documents, birth and marriage certificates, and prepared a genealogy of our family in case we were asked for this information. While he did this, he changed the names of some of our ancestors which he thought did not sound French enough. Everyone in our family became Catholic except one of his grandparents who became a methodist, a humorous bit, since most French officials would not know what a methodist was.

Our family continued to ignore Vichy's antisemitic decrees and con-tinued throughout 1940-42 to prune and harvest our roses the same way Voltaire's hero Candide, continued to cultivate his garden during another war. This was not because we did not care about what was happening in our country, but because we thought it was the best way to survive and help others.

Throughout my life I never could accept the persecution of anyone for his or her religious beliefs, but the persecution of someone for the beliefs of his or her ancestors, as the Nazis carried it out, was not only abhorrent to me, but did not make any sense. Discriminating against people who have opinions differing from yours is called political discrimination. Discriminating against people whom you consider biologically different from you is what has been called racial discrimination. Though I deplore both types of discrimination, I have to make a distinction between them. In the first case, one chooses to be a freemason, a socialist, or a communist and it is possible, in order to survive, to temporarily abandon one's own ideas and adopt those of the enemy. But, as for the second case, one does not choose to be the child or the grandchild of a Jew. Yet, the individual with such a family background in Nazi Europe was marked as expendable and doomed. In the same way, no one chooses the color of his or her skin, but in South Africa and in the United States, for an individual with dark skin, there is no escape: he or she is marked and generally discriminated against throughout his or her life.

Although I had some Jewish ancestors, I never considered myself a Jew. I certainly could not accept either the Berlin or Vichy definition of a Jew. I could not understand why someone with Jewish grandparents, yet raised as a Christian, as some of my friends were, or someone like me, who had never been brought up in any religion, could be considered to be a Jew. For me, the religious adherence of some of my ancestors to the Jewish faith or any other faith had nothing to do with me. What I believed was far more relevant to me than what my parents or my ancestors believed. In my unsophisticated mind, as a teenager, I assumed that religion had something to do with antisemitism. But in fact, as I discovered later, it has very little to do with it. It is a smokescreen concealing something that lies deep in the minds of many of us.

It is a natural thing for us to blame someone other than ourselves when things go wrong and when times are tough. Jews, who have usually been an easily identified minority wherever they happened to be, have been the perpetual scapegoats. They have been blamed for everything: for the death of Christ, the occurrence of pestilence and sexual diseases, and for the evils of communism as well as capitalism. It has occurred to me that if there were only two old and senile Jews in a town, they would be held responsible for all the misery occurring in that town. In 1940, the Jews were now held responsible for the defeat of France. Time had come to deal with the Jews. But even if it were true that some Jewish politicians were responsible for the defeat, no government worthy of the name would hold an entire class of people guilty for the actions of a few individuals.

Yet, within days of taking office, the first Pétain cabinet sealed the borders to prevent anyone from leaving France without official permission. Shortly after that it cancelled the April 1939 law that had forbidden antisemitic statements in the press. It then established a panel to review the naturalization of foreigners. This was done in order to revoke citizenship previously granted not only to Jewish immigrants, but also to non-Jewish immigrants who were political enemies of the new regime. At the same time Vichy issued decrees facilitating the internment of foreign Jews and withdrawing citizenship from the Jews in Algeria.

Both French and German antisemitism was not based on religion, but on biology or rather pseudobiology, This type of antisemitism, which was not invented by Hitler but was carried to the extreme by him, was based upon the mythical concept of pure races. Racists, such as Hitler, assumed that groups (pure races) of human beings who were more or less similar in their physical and moral qualities existed not just in the distant past but also in the present. They assumed also that some of these groups (races) were superior to others.

It was only later, as a trained biologist, that I understood the basic flaws of Nazi antisemitism. There have never been any pure races, for groups of people have never been isolated long enough to become human beings of only one type. Since time immemorial there has always been breeding among human groups. This is why, wherever you go, you find extreme diversity among the inhabitants of a city or even a village. When you are in Berlin or Oslo you will not find just tall, blond, blue eyed people, but also short black-haired, brown-eyed individuals and many individuals who cannot be classified.

In general racists of today, as those in the past, believe in the myth that allowing races to mix will destroy the superior ones. Thus, members of inferior races should not be allowed to interbreed with members of the superior races. This belief is based on another myth, namely the idea that heredity is transmitted by blood, which, as a fluid, mingles and blends in the children. According to this myth, good and bad qualities are transmitted through blood. Hence, the blood of the inferior races, considered inpure, should not be mixed with the blood of the master race which in itself is pure. A drop of blood of an "inferior" individual is enough to taint the blood of a "superior" individual. Accordingly, someone who has a Jewish ancestor, no matter how many generations back, is a Jew, since one drop of blood from this ancestral Jew is enough to taint the blood of all his descendents. The same is true for a black person or a Gypsy.

Science has taught us that blood has many properties, but transmission of heredity is not one of them. Even during Hitler's time we already knew that heredity was not transmitted by blood, but by genes whose expression depends upon the environment in which the organism develops. The physical and mental development of a human being depends on the interaction of that person's genes and the environment in which he or she lives. Therefore, a child from Chinese parents raised in Shanghai is not expected to behave the same way than if it was raised in New York.

Science has taught us that "bad or good" qualities are not carried in the blood as Hitler wanted us to believe, nor are they carried by genes as modern racists want us to believe. Science has also taught us that behavioral traits are not linked to physical traits, destroying another tenet of racism, namely that the greater the physical differences between the ingroup, the master race, and a given outgroup, the more inferior the outgroup is.

Science also teaches us that two individuals of the same family but several generations apart are uncorrelated in their genetic constitution. If you tell an historian or social scientist that you are a descendant of Benjamin Franklin, he or she may attach some importance to this fact. However, if you say this to a geneticist, he or she will regard this information as irrelevant to your own biological worth, for you and Mr. Franklin have nothing in common except that you are two human beings. So, even if it were true that Jews are biologically different from other people, the fact that you have Jewish ancestors somewhere in your distant past has no scientific meaning.

To determine the race of someone, as the Nazis did, by the number of practicing Jews in his or her family is committing extreme violence not only against science, but also against common sense. But this, of course, has never stopped doctrines like racism from flourishing.

After many years of studying and teaching genetics, I had the scientific answer to the question that bothered me during my teen age years, namely what is a Jew? The answer was the same as the one I formulated when I was a young man, that Jews are not a race and that the only valid criterion for determining membership in the group is confessional (adherence to the Jewish faith). Unfortunately, in spite of advances in genetics, the view that the Jews are a race has persisted until today among both Jews and non-Jews. Although this view, rooted far in the past, has been scientifically discredited, it is still very widespread. Is this a consequence of Hitler's propaganda, still flourishing fifty years after his death or are there other reasons inherent in human nature? Is it basically a distrust of people who are not like us? Will racism ever be eradicated from human minds?

I don't know. What I do know is that one of its most frightening aspects is that it seems to act as a slow virus attacking its unsuspecting victims. Once it lodges in their minds, it prevents them from seeing their fellow human beings as individuals. Rather they see them as members of a group. I think there are two forms of the virus; one mild, the other deadly. In the case of the mild form, the victims do not realize that they are stereotytping. How many times have I heard: "But you are French! You should..." Being French born, I was supposed to drink wine and be an excellent lover like Charles Boyer or be able to sing like Maurice Chevalier. But if the virus mutates to the deadly form, it leads to the most blatant type of racism. The victims of this deadly viral form do not see mankind as a whole, but as separate races, destined to fight each other until one, supposedly the physically and mentally superior, is victorious.

Facing a vicious and deadly antisemitism, the "Jews" in France were torn like Hamlet, whose famous soliloquy can be paraphrased as:

To fight or not to fight: that was the question; Whether it was wiser to suffer in silence The slings and arrows of outrageous fortune, Or to take arms against a sea of troubles,...

They took two extreme positions. I am using the word Jew here as defined by the Nazis, that is as anyone who had some Jewish ancestry as far back as two generations. A minority of them, reacted the same way as my parents did and took their first step toward fighting the Nazis, by rewriting their family tree and by changing the names and religious affiliations of their ancestors. In this way many were able to survive the holocaust.

Other "Jews" were unable to persuade themselves that their lives were at stake. They thought they could be saved by strictly adhering to German and Vichy antisemitic rules and believed that, as long as they did what was asked of them, no real harm could come to them. They hoped that each turn of the screw was the last one, believing that there were rational limits to this barbarous persecution. They could not be convinced by any-one, not even by their own kin, that for Hitler the Final Solution to the Jewish question was death to all Jews and that any document signed by a Nazi was not worth the paper it was written on. They believed that in the country of Liberty, Fraternity and Equality, it was unthinkable that Jews whose families had been in France for many years, would be prevented from working and shopping with the rest of the population, would have to ride in the last car of the metro, would be kicked out of their homes and deported to death camps. They did not believe that this could happen to them and when they were asked to declare themselves as Jews at the Prefecture of Police they did. When they got I.D. Cards with the word, JUIF OR JUIVE, (JEW) written across them, they carried these cards with them. When they were asked to wear the yellow star in the occupied zone, they did. Finally, when they were ordered to leave their homes and their possessions behind and to enter the cattle cars, it was too late. They went like sheep to a slaughterhouse. They went to their death having underestimated both the insanity of the Nazis and the capacity of some of their countrymen for betrayal.

There were of course a lot of "Jews" who had started to obey the Nazi decrees, but when they saw restrictions and prohibitions proliferating until life itself became impossible, they decided that they should fight back. And so they did-in any way they could.

In these dreadful times it was obvious that, if one were to survive, one did not obey any governmental decree which would jeopardize one's life, but also that one had to modify one's behavior so as not to attract public attention to oneself. Unfortunately, it seemed that many people had a very hard time doing this.

For instance, I remember two orthodox Jewish friends of mine, a teen age girl and her brother, who could not abandon their ingrained traditions. Gilles and I were with them up in the Alps one summer day. It was around noon and we were very hungry. Our young friends had very little to eat. Gilles and I, more fortunate, had some ham sandwiches that we offered to share with them. But our friends refused to eat them. The seventeen year old girl patiently explained to us that Jews did not eat pork. I tried, but to no avail, to convince them that God would forgive them, for in order to survive, they had to find food wherever they could. That same day I found out that both of our friends were carrying I.D. cards with the word JEW printed on them in large letters. Again I stressed the idea that in order to survive it would be to their advantage to have cards without such an obvious red flagging word. This time the brother told us jokingly that he could not possibly get rid of such a card, for sooner or later, the liberation of France would come and everyone would have to prove that he or she was not a collaborator. The card that he had would be a proof that he was not a friend of the Nazis. It seemed to me that our friends were fighting fire with fire. Yet, they were never arrested. They were lucky, for by 1943 the fate of the Jews, whether they were French or Foreign, was sealed. Except for a few who by sheer luck did not fall into the hands of the Gestapo, those who declared themselves or were recognized as Jews, regardless of age, sex, or political affiliations were sooner or later condemned to death. Under Hitler's orders, Jews had to be exterminated and that was that. For practical purposes, the "Jews" who escaped the holocaust were those who did not accept the orders given by Vichy or Berlin. They did not register or if they did, they disappeared under assumed names within the French population, hiding somewhere with the help of their countrymen. This was far easier for children to do than for adults for they could work on farms where their labor was desperately needed. Quite a few young "Jewish" men and women ended up fighting in the underground while others escaped from occupied Europe by various routes.

PART 5

SURVIVAL IN UNOCCUPIED FRANCE

Chapter 10

The Quest For Food

Hitler exploited the people's continuing need for food to gain the physi-cal services of millions of workers in the countries that he had conquered.
TONY MARCH IN DARKNESS OVER EUROPE.

If our family was ever to see the liberation of France it was obviously necessary for us to survive until then. To do this we needed food which became more and more scarce as months passed. Though France has always been known for its richness in agricultural products, by 1941 there was already a shortage of food, especially in the cities. This was due to two factors. One was that the British navy prevented the shipment of food by sea from the French colonies and therefore we were isolated. The second factor was more important. The German government was taking a lot of food products out of France to feed, not just its soldiers, but also its civilian population. Ironically, it was paying us for all these products with money that it extracted from us for the privilege of governing us. The amount of money was considerable, 400,000,000 francs or $80,000,000 a month. Because of this leaching the franc depreciated more rapidly in 1940-1944 than the currency of any other Western European country except Italy. With this money, the Germans became the main clients of the black market, buying food, drinks, and clothing. The Germans systemat-ically plundered the French countryside to feed their armed forces and their people at home. Day after day, convoys of trucks rolled eastward carrying cattle and corn, wool and wine, and coal leaving the French cold and hungry. The next four years were to be the four leanest, bitterest years that the French people would experience in this century. There is no doubt that the fate of the newborns was the most tragic as many young mothers who were underfed could not nurse their babies and having no access to condensed milk were forced to watch their babies starve to death, help-less to save them.

Food was rationed. Coupons allowed us to receive no more than 200 grams of fats such as oil and butter, and 300 grams of meat per person per month. This amounted to less than half a pound of each class of food. Potatoes and vegetables were also distributed sparingly. All this represented at the most food for five days out of the month. Teenagers were slightly favored. They had J3 coupons which permitted them to have a little more meat, sugar, and fatty substances than the normal adult citizen. But, in fact, they were always hungry and it was not unusual for adults, their parents or friends to give their meat portions to them. People were known to tie up a piece of meat at the end of a string and let it float in boiling water for a few minutes to give flavor to a vegetable soup and then withdraw the meat to be used again.

In fact, however, the system of rationing soon became almost meaningless because the coupons could not be honored. Women would stand in line all day for just a single loaf of bread which usually had more wood pulp in it than wheat flour, or for something they hoped was edible. Soap, a pat of real butter, a cup of real coffee soon became luxuries beyond the reach of all but a tiny minority. A book could be written on substances that were tried in vain as substitutes for coffee. Everything from roasted and ground oak acorns to fruit pits were used, but believe me, there is no substitute for real coffee.

The department of Alpes Maritimes in which we lived had very little arable land and therefore little food could be produced locally to feed its population. People became obsessed with the problem of surviving, and in fact some did not survive. No wonder that Frenchmen, if rich enough, resorted to buying on the black market. In some ways our family was more fortunate than others who lived in the cities. We were living on a farm, and though meat was very scarce, we ate a lot of vegetables that we grew. We also grew crops like lentils, generally not grown along the French Riviera because the weather is too warm. The production was meager, but we were able to eat some lentils. We were able to raise a few rabbits and we had olive oil to exchange for food.

The raising of rabbits was my brother's job and mine. Every morning before going to school we had to find some rabbit food: grass and weeds, inedible vegetable remains from our kitchen (if any). From time to time we had to clean the messy cages. And in order to have the right matings in the appropriate cages we had to become experts in recognizing the sex of these prolific bunnies. Finally, we had also to overcome our sensibilities and be able to kill these gentle animals. But, when one is hungry, one transcends those human feelings of compassion, and in this case, one has to see a rabbit as the piece de resistance of a delicious meal. Our first execution though turned out to be a disaster. We were supposed to kill the rabbit with one stroke of a big stick in the back of the neck. We missed and I still remember the poor animal, still fully alive, looking at us with his moon eyes that seemed to ask what are you jerks, trying to do? We managed to kill him and became better at this necessary job. Unfortunately, within a few months a viral disease spread through our rabbits, and in spite of our all efforts we lost every one of them.

As to our olive oil, it came from our property of Clair Matin at Roquebrune. There we had 100 very old and tall olive trees. Before the war we did not harvest any of their olives because at that time it did not pay to harvest and crush the olives, extracting the oil from them. However, during the war years there was a shortage of fatty substances, including olive oil. All of sudden our olive trees became vital to improving our lot. It was impossible for us to personally be at Roquebrune, because it had become part of Italy and French people had been evicted. However, the Profumo family, who had been working on our farm since 1932, was Italian and being Italian was allowed to remain on our farm throughout the war years. The Profumos harvested all the olives that they could get and gave us half of the oil production. We used part of it to cook with and to make soap. Father became a chemist, managing to manufacture bar soaps that smelled a bit like the palmolive kind. We bartered the rest of our olive oil for things that we needed and could not get otherwise butter, bread and even wool to make sweaters.

In spite of the fact that we had a lot of things that urban families did not have, our devoted mother passed a lot of time getting food for her family. She used to ride to town on her bicycle with baskets hanging on each side of the back wheel. However, she never paid any attention to the state of health of her bicycle, that we named "Becassine" after a famous cartoon character. Becassine was a stupid girl to whom all kinds of unfortunate things happened. One day we saw Mother coming home with Becassine's front wheel wobbling terribly. We checked the wheel and found that the nuts on the axle were completely loose. We tightened them thinking how lucky our Mother was not to have gotten into a terrible accident.

In the Summer of 1942 Mother, who then was 50, was very tired and asked the former maid to Uncle Fernand to come and help her for a few months. This lady who was in her late thirties was what my parents called a pearl. She could do everything well: cooking, cleaning house, washing. But she had a special gift. Not only could she repair clothes, but she could make them. She should have had her own shop, but circumstances had been such that she never could realize her dream. Her name was Isabel. She was born in Spain, in the Basque province of Guspicosa. She came to France and married a man who was the valet of my Uncle Fernand. Isabel's husband, Thomas Assin, had the sad experience of passing five years of his life from 1940 to 1945 in a prison camp. He was liberated by the Russians, but not before he had a taste of life under the communists, which he did not appreciate at all. He told me later that there had been two things he could not stand, eating millet and being checked by a female physician. It was a pleasure to have Isabel with us during that Summer. In the fall she returned to her apartment in Pau where she hid a Jewish couple for months. We heard later from her that, though she had wanted to help them, she had little respect for this particular couple who did nothing to help her during their stay in her apartment.

Chapter 11

Work And Fun In Antibes

Mens sane in corpore sano

Gilles and I worked a lot on our parents' farm in Antibes, tending to the vegetables, taking care of the roses, watering and pruning them. Pruning roses is as art that I learned from an old man, just as I did the art of making uncemented stone terraces from Old Fratini back at Roquebrune. I was taught how to choose the healthy newly grown stems and cut them just above the two lower buds. All the weak small stems had to be cut off for I was told they only eat the sap of the bush without giving us any good roses. Pruning roses made me feel like a god, for I had to decide in a split moment which stems were to stay and live and which stems were to be cut and die. I never forgot how to prune roses and I can say with pride that many rose gardens have been beautified by my own work or with my advice. We painted the greenhouses, replaced broken window glass-another useful thing I learned as a young man, and since this time I have always repaired broken windows myself in any building I own.

One of our main jobs on the farm was to haul the baskets of flowers to the railway station. Since there was no gasoline during these war years, we had to transport everything by bicycle, including the hauling of the flower baskets. They were put into a light home made trailer which was hitched to our bicycles, and every two days off we went, Gilles and I, bicycling to the railway station located about two miles from our home. This velo- trailer means of locomotion replaced Father's Model A Ford, the back of which opened like the gate of future station wagons, to carry the numerous carnation baskets.

The story of this Model A Ford, which we called "La Rouge" because of its outstanding red color, should be told, for no other car I have known was ever built to last like this one. Father, hoping that some day gasoline would be plentiful, hid our model A under ten feet of carnation baskets. To be sure that no one would steal it he took the wheels off and the battery out and carried them to a friend's home. When liberation came four years later, he put the tires back on "La Rouge", installed the battery and called the local Ford Garage to have the car towed and checked. He was asked if he had started the engine. Father had not, for who would believe that after four years the car would start on its own. But it did after Father cranked the engine. Our Model A took off and Father went to the garage to be told that everything was fine. Father did not drive the car too much after the liberation, for there still was little gasoline to be had. In 1950 when my parents decided to immigrate to the United States, Father sold "La Rouge" to a young man in town. This young man had never had a car and did not know that one should put oil in the crankcase from time to time and soon he ruined the engine. What an inglorious death for such a marvelous car. Father should have kept it as an antique, a tribute to Quality One of the Ford Motor Company.

Gilles and I studied diligently at school, worked hard on the farm, but also had fun. During the spring of 1942 Father gave us a small boat, about 12 feet long and 3 feet wide, with only one sail. He thought that it would be fun for his two boys to have a boat. But there was also a practical reason for his gift: he thought that we would use it to go fishing. With luck we should be able to have some sea food to put on the table. We did get fish. However, not with fishing rods, but rather by a new method called goggle diving. Goggle diving preceded scubba diving which would be invented and introduced by Captain Jacques Cousteau in 1943, a year after Gilles and I took up goggle diving.

The idea of swimming, diving and doing all kinds of things underwater was very challenging to us. How could we do this? We needed a watertight glass mask through which we could see and a snorkel tube to breath through as we floated face down in the water admiring sea landscapes or spotting fish below. We also needed some means to kill a fish if we ever saw one. Since at that time there was no equipment of that sort you could buy, we had to make it ourselves or have it made. And this is what we did. The mask was cut out of a large tire innertube, the front being framed by an aluminum circle used for closing large glass jars. Two rubber gas-stove hoses were inserted into the sides of the mask. In order to prevent water from getting into our mask when diving, two ping pong balls were inserted into the hoses, but in order to prevent the ping pong balls from falling off the hoses into the water, two reed rods of the right diameter were inserted into the end of each rubber hose. This mask permitted us to dive with ease.

This primitive snorkel was not too hard to make and certainly was not expensive. However, we had to turn to a professional for the next piece of equipment, the fishing gun or rather the long slingshot. It consisted of a broom stick. On the front end of the stick was fastened an arrow with a hook. This arrow had to be made by a blacksmith and was the most expensive part of our equipment. The broomstick was propelled by a long narrow strip of rubber, cut out of an innertube. Both ends of the rubber strip were attached to the back end of the broom stick. The folded strip of rubber was half as long as the broomstick. To propel our homemade slingshot, we put our wrist through the fold of the rubber strip, then gripped the front end of the broomstick as far as the rubber strip permitted us. When we saw a prey, we let go of the broomstick which did not go far; nor fast. But it worked, for fish did not hear or see the broomstick under water coming toward them.

Though we had not heard of Frederic Dumas, Captain Cousteau's colleague, known as the best goggle diver of France, we were using more or less his technique to dive. We were bending from the waist and pointing the head and torso down. Then we would throw our legs up in the air with a powerful snap and down we would go. Though we were not as good as Dumas, who could go down to sixty feet- our record was only around thirty feet- we had lots of fun seeing under water. A few times we were actually able to add some sea food to our dinner table, a real treat for the whole family.

With our boat we were able to inspect every nook and cranny along the Cap d'Antibes. One day we came inside a little beach belonging to the the famous resort, Villa-Eden Roc, with its swimming-pool which used to glitter with Hollywood stars. Someone on the rocks was yelling to us that this was a private beach. And private it was, for, to our astonishment, we saw a woman and a man, without a stitch on, swimming without shame around our boat. This was our first experience at seeing nudists on a beach. We left slowly with the wind blowing in the sail.

Being teenagers is a difficult period of life, for it is the time of dawning sexual awareness. It is the time when boys consciously or unconsciously want to impress girls. Gilles and I were no exception. One day the chance to show off materialized. From the beach we saw some girls sunbathing on the top of the limestone rocks that edged the beach of Juan Les Pins overhanging the sea. We climbed to where the beauties were lying, then we ran along past them and impulsively dove into the sea. It seemed to us that our descent through the air was taking quite a while. Later we found that we were right, for we had dived from close to fifty feet. We were fortunate. We were all-right except for our faces and necks which took a beating. We obviously succeeded beyond our imagination to impress the girls, for they jumped to their feet and made it in time to the cliff's edge to see us surface. I suppose that the young ladies were impressed not so much by our athletic abilities, but by our stupidity for not having realized how high those rocks were. In any case we never jumped from them again.

That same summer there were many people swimming or sun-bathing on the beach and one thing happened which has stuck in my memory until today. As it always seems to be, there is always a bully in every crowd. This particular bully was a ten year old boy, whose pleasure it was to keep the heads of younger children under the water until they practically suffocated. He did this to maybe two or three young boys. In my mind I still can see a man of about forty jumping in the water at full speed, picking up the bully in the air and slamming him under the water, keeping him there for at least a minute. Once released, the bully surfaced blue, purple, and shaking all over. After a few minutes he walked back to the beach, crying and calling for his mother. As the man sat on the beach with his own children we applauded him for having taught this young bully his lesson. It seems that French fathers do not fear to teach the right behavior to children other than their own.

Chapter 12

Rough Times For Our Family And Friends

What is freedom? the knowledge that if someone knocks at your door at 5.00 A.M. it is the milkman and not the Gestapo.

A COUSIN OF THE AUTHOR

We were surviving, but what about the rest of our family? Some members were like us in unoccupied France, others were under the German occupation. Father's sister, Emma, and youngest brother, Henry, lived in Hyères, a town on the French Riviera, not very far from Antibes. We not only heard from them, but they visited us and we visited them. My mother's youngest sister, Odette, also lived with her husband and her three sons in the unoccupied zone in the town of Chateauroux and we heard from her also. However, it was very hard to obtain news from the rest of our family who lived in Paris, separated from us by the line of demarcation which acted as a true sealed frontier. We were not allowed to write letters, but sent postcards purchased from the post office. These astonishing cards were preprinted with bland statements such as I am well, I am not well. We simply crossed out the messages that did not apply.

Things were so bad in Paris in 1941 that some members of our family decided to cross the demarcation line and come into the unoccupied zone. In the Spring of 1941 our aging maternal grandmother moved from Paris to Chateauroux to be with her youngest daughter. There were many ways that one could cross the demarcation line, all of them dangerous. You could take the train, but if you did not have the right authorization to do this, chances were that you would be arrested or at least turned back. You could walk across the line, but you risked of course being arrested by border patrols. Grandmother, being too old to walk across the border was transported inside a garbage truck in a special container within the garbage. I never knew the details of the trip, but it was successful as she safely reached her daughter's home. She only lived there a few months though as she died in September of natural causes and surrounded by two of her five daughters.

Only months later one of my cousins, called Jean Claude, also crossed the line of demarcation at the same spot that Grandmother did. But being young and daring he crossed the line on a motorcycle. One of his friends was a physician who had patients on both sides of the line. He had obtained a permit from the Germans which allowed him to cross the line whenever necessary. When the planned day of escape arrived, the physician told Jean Claude to climb on the back of his motorcycle and they would cross the line together. Jean Claude was to play the part of a physician. He donned a white frock and put a stethoscope around his neck. He did not need it, however, to hear his own heart beat when they were stopped at the border. The physician told the Germans that Jean Claude was his associate whom he needed for his expertise in order to treat a patient. Jean Claude was not asked for his papers, which was a very good thing because he did not have any. He was a very lucky man. A few days later he joined us in Antibes, passed a few months with us helping us on the farm, and soon disappeared, where I have no idea. Later we learned that during the winter of 1942 he crossed the Spanish Border with a group of friends. Some of them froze to death at high elevations, but Jean Claude, lucky as usual, suffered only from frost bite that affected two of his toes. When he reached North Africa he enlisted in the Free French Forces and was trained as a paratrooper. Later in 1944 he parachuted into Belgium during the battle of the Bulge. Out of 130 of his unit two men survived. He was one of them.

Early in the summer of 1942 another cousin of ours, eight months younger than I came to live with us. His name was Francis. Until then, he had lived in Paris with his mother, a single parent. She decided that it had become too dangerous for her only son to stay there and had asked my parents to take care of him. Francis completely shared our fate during the occupation. He became a brother to us and has remained one throughout our lives.

That same summer, we learned first hand about how far the persecution of the Jews by Hitler had gone. We knew of course that they were persecuted and many of them arrested, but we had no details. We learned how bad the situation was from a young man who was a friend of Francis. We were at the beach of Juan Les Pins one afternoon, when Francis saw one of his former schoolmates who was Jewish. The young man told us about his escape from the Gare de l'Est, one of the four Paris railway stations.

He had been arrested and put in one of these infamous cattle cars. The Germans had packed the train with hundreds of Jews, Arabs, Blacks and Gypsies. Its destination was Poland. There was no food, no water and a only a few buckets for human waste. It was the beginning of the holocaust, the horror of which nobody at the time could imagine. Yet Francis' young friend had a gut feeling that this trip meant death for all of the people in the train. He looked up and saw that the only window, in the roof of the railway car, was open. He immediately thought of escaping. So he asked a young Arab to help him to reach that window. The Arab told him that he would surely be shot by the German soldier who was standing half way through the door with a machine gun. Francis' friend answered that they were going to be killed anyway and escape was their only possible way out. He was a very good gymnast; muscular and daring. He climbed up on the shoulders of his newly found friend and reached the window. He made one of these muscle-ups for which the gymnasts are famous, and immediately was on the roof of the railway car. As he attempted to slide down he was seen by the railway engineer of a locomotive on the next track. The engineer gestured to him to go under the locomotive and indicated that he would stop just long enough for our friend to pass under it. That is what the young man did. He then climbed up on the platform and melted into the crowd. Managing to reach the apartment of a friend, he took a well needed shower and ate a well deserved steak meal, for he had not eaten for three days. Under another identity he managed to reach the French Riviera where we met him. He was looking for a way to escape from France and join the Allied Forces. We never saw him after this.

Two of our cousins, Pierre and Ginette, died during the occupation. Pierre, a medical student, was picked up by the Germans at his home in the early morning hours on a cold day in February in 1942. He was sent to the Russian front as a medic and never came back. The young woman, Ginette, who worked for the underground, was arrested by the Gestapo. We believe she died of pneumonia and dehydration in the concentration camp of Drancy. Her parents also died in a concentration camp sometime in 1943. So did Francis' mother. I never knew the details of their arrests. Out of 36 direct members of our family 31 survived the German occupation of France.

Chapter 13

Resistance and Our Family

Frenchmen, do not grumble because the curfew starts at 9.P.M. This is necessary for it allows you to listen to the BBC.

Soon after the 1940 armistice the Resistance movement was started on a very small scale by individuals and groups whose philosophies were very different from each other, such as Christian democrats, military officers, and communists. The presence of the latter in the underground has to be explained. From June 1940 to June 1941, communists were tolerated and even protected by the Germans in occupied France because the Soviets were at the time the Allies of the Germans. But in non-occupied France they were arrested by the Vichy police and thrown in jail. After June 1941, when Germany invaded the Soviet Union, they became passionate and efficient resisters.

There were few resisters in 1940. The rest of the population was extremely passive. These early resisters had little or no experience in what opposition to a totalitarian government might involve, but they shared an urge and determination to do something without always knowing what it was they could do or should do. Acting in individualistic ways they stood against the passivity of Vichy-France and in defiance of the 1940 capitulation, often in apparent contradiction to their own political positions or public image before the war. They frequently surprised their countrymen and not infrequently surprised themselves, for their refusal to accept what was offered in 1940 then looked absurd. Fortunately for them and for France, their refusal became more rational and sensible as time passed.

If there was a commonality in the character of resisters of the first hour it was one of personality. They were men and women with strong convictions that they were right. They had a strong feeling of patriotism, but this did not explain entirely why they chose to resist. May be they were more clear-sighted, less submissive, less concerned with day-to-day survival, more imaginative and more independent than their countrymen. Some might have been influenced by family or educational connections with England or America; others by their personal experience in the war, having been injured, or taken as prisoners, or having fought fascism already in the 1930's. For some, their family situations drove them to join, or think of joining, the underground.

This seemed to have been my case. I found myself discriminated against for having Jewish ancestors I never even knew. But being discriminated against does not automatically lead someone to fight back. After all, as with French society at large in 1940, only a small minority of Jews eventually responded to the Vichy regime with outright opposition. As for me, I was raised in a pacifist family. Why should I want to fight and risk my life? Though I never thought there was any reason to fight the Germans in 1914, I was sure that there had been one excellent one to fight them in 1939, or even sooner. It was to get rid of Hitler and his Nazi clique. Germany was led by a madman, a liar and a killer. He killed not only Jews, but also Catholics, Gypsies, mental defectives, and prison inmates. Like dictators before him and after him, Hitler assassinated not only his political enemies but many of his former friends who put him in power. By 1937 Germany had become a world turned upside down where decent people were in concentration camps and criminals were in charge of the police and judicial courts. This social madness had spread to Austria by 1938, Czechoslovakia and Poland by 1939, to Belgium, Holland, Denmark, Luxembourg and France by 1940.

We knew that Hitler's racial philosophy was the dominant force of his power, but we did not know that it was also a symptom of his mental derangement. According to his own entourage, Hitler could not separate in his mind the Jewish question from war plans. He is reported to have made very fine distinctions among categories of half-jews in the middle of an important discussion of how to invade Austria. Later, when his armies were retreating from France, all the French trains should have been used to carry troops and material, but they were not. Hitler had given the priority of requisitioning trains to the Gestapo, not the Army. This was done so that more Jews could be carried to gas chambers instead of bringing troops back to Germany. Two weeks before Hitler committed suicide, he wrote a note urging his followers to carry out the "final solution" after his death. Why did Hitler hate the Jews so much? It is still not clear. Was his paternal grandfather a Jew who abandoned his family as some people suggested? Was he refused entrance to art academies because of Jewish directors as others have suggested? Whatever the reason, the world was faced with a madman who, like Stalin, was responsible for the death of millions of people. Hitler's madness had to be stopped.

Though it was obvious that I could do little to reverse the trend, it was clear to me that in order to keep my sanity I had to do something. I did not have to look very far to find contacts in the Resistance. One of my schoolmates, Alain Cianfanelli, though only fifteen years old, was a spy for the British Intelligence Service. I was one of the few he trusted and our friendship played an important part during these troubled times. He knew that secrets were safe with me. One day he told me with pride that he had been able to discover that one member of the British Intelligence was a double agent. He had communicated his finding to London and the agent was arrested in Turkey and taken care of.

In these troubled times to be able to trust someone was very important, for it was a true life and death decision. If you were wrong in your judgment, you risked betrayal, arrest, and even death. There were innumerable cases of betrayal among the resisters. There were even cases of Jews being betrayed by other Jews. How did you know whether or not you could trust a specific person? You could not read his or her inner thoughts as you read a clock on the wall. You could not simply rely on luck. Maybe there was something in the way the person looked at you, something in his or her eyes that drove you to open your own thoughts. Maybe there was something in the way that person talked to you that made you trust him or her. Of course you might be right or wrong, but this is also true in our choice of mates. After all we do not know for sure that they love us. How many times have we been fooled? Of course, the differences between a mistake in the choice of a marriage partner and a mistake in the choice of a comrade in the underground was that the former led to less serious consequences than the latter. Our family was very lucky. No one ever betrayed us.

I expressed to Alain Cianfanelli my desire to serve in the Resistance, but he told me that for the time being his network had all the agents it needed. It was believed, and rightly so, that the effectiveness of the Resistance was inversely proportional to its popularization. The less people knew about the details of what the Resistance was doing, the less the Germans would be able to interfere. However, if I wanted, I could be part of the second wave. What he meant by that was that, in the case of the death or the disappearance of many of these agents, I would be contacted by a certain Dr. Levy, a local physician, and be accepted as a member of their network. Dr. Levy, known under the name of Louis, played a very important role in the underground. He was a member of the Special Operations Executive or SOE for short. The SOE, a British secret military organization, was created by Winston Churchill on 19 July 1940. Its objective was "to coordinate all action by way of subversion and sabotage against the enemy overseas." Dr. Levy was in charge of secret submarine landings on the French Riviera, many of them just off the Antibes harbor. Thanks to these landings, many important agents and political figures came and left France safely. Eventually Dr.Levy was arrested by the Gestapo, and murdered as he was transferred from one place to another.

I never joined Dr.Levy's underground's network, but a few times I was asked to do something for the Resistance. For instance, one day in 1942, I was told to listen to the BBC for a special message. Throughout all the war years the BBC sent special messages which had meaning only for special groups of the underground or the resistance fighters. For example, the message could have been something like "the frogs croaked during the Spring". In that case it would have meant that an airplane would land the next night in a special location and the underground fighters there should be ready to act. Listening to the BBC. was a ritual for us. Like many other Frenchmen we crowded around the radio, cautiously turning the knobs trying to hear every word of the broadcast which was jammed by the Germans. Well, that particular night I heard the expected message. I had no idea of its meaning but I called my friend Alain to tell him that I heard it.

As I listened to the BBC that particular night a family secret was revealed to me. Henry, my father's younger brother, was at our home in Antibes, listening with me to the same BBC broadcast. He reacted to the message the same way that I did. I bluntly asked him if he knew what the message meant. The way he did not answer the question, I knew he was part of the underground. I told him his secret was safe with me. It remained so. Only after the liberation did Father learn what his younger brother had done during the war years. Working as a civilian secretary for the French Vichy Army, Uncle Henry had duplicated numerous secret documents that had to do with the transport of German troops along the Mediterranean coast. For this work he was later decorated by Charles de Gaulle.

There is no doubt that our survival during these troubled years was due to our mother's devotion to getting food for her family and to our father's foresight in politics. It was very clear to him that in order for the four of us to remain alive he was not going to obey any rule dictated by the Vichy Government which was not only violently antisemitic but also antiparliamentary and antimasonic, and against freedom. Father's contribution to the resistance was to be in helping his family, family members, and friends, to get new identities so they would not be caught by the Vichy police. He got involved in this patriotic forgery very early after the armistice.

French people, in peace-time as well as in war-time, have to carry identity cards which state their name, residence, birth date, birthplace, profession, and give a physical description. The cards can be asked for at any time by the police. The American reader might think that this policy is one of a police state, but French people do not seem to mind it. They use their ID cards in the same way that the Americans use their driver's licenses. This question of individual freedom is an interesting one. American Universities which I attended have officially asked me my religion, a question that I find very personal and in some way offensive. No French governmental agency (except under Vichy) ever dared to ask the religion of anyone. Under Vichy the only citizens whose religion was recorded were the Jews. But it was possible for them to avoid these cards if they did not register as Jews, if their name was not Jewish sounding, if their neighbors and associates did not know they were Jewish, or if they did they chose not to divulge it, and if, of course, they did not publicly practice their faith.

Father was much aware of the importance of blending into the setting, not to attract attention to oneself, and he was always on the lookout for ways to prevent trouble for himself and his family. One day he made an interesting remark: "When policemen check identity cards on buses, they never ask the driver to show his. Maybe "he added," I should be a bus driver." Could it be that policemen did not believe a Jew could drive a bus? After all for many years in the United States people did not believe that "Blacks" could fly a plane.

It took great courage for Father to start actively resisting the Vichy edicts, but courage begets itself and soon he got involved in manufacturing false identity cards. This involvement came after a meeting that he had at the City Hall with a young man who used to be a policeman at Roquebrune, but now was a policeman at Antibes. Among the many duties that my father had in Roquebrune as vice- mayor was giving aptitude tests to candidates for police work. One of them had been this very policeman who was now at Antibes.

Father talked with him a lot about the good old days and renewed their friendship which paid off a few months later when some of our relatives needed false identification cards. Father thought that this policeman friend of his could help. He went to the City Hall and bluntly told him what he needed. What he needed from him was not much really, just the rubber stamp of the police station. Father would fill in all the details on blank ID cards and sign for the police commissioner. But he needed the rubber stamp. The policeman wanted to help Father, but having never done anything of that sort before he was reluctant to stamp a false ID. Finally, he gave Father a blank ID and told him that he would be back a few minutes later. What he did was to go to the w.c., giving Father time to use the rubber stamp. If later it were discovered that the ID was forged, the policeman could only be charged with stupidity. That day, Father got the card he wanted. No one discovered what they had done. And, in fact, later our friendly patriotic policeman made false ID cards not only for our family but for others. After the liberation of France he came back to Roquebrune very proud of his underground work. After all, he had been part of a minority of policemen who did not carry out the orders of the Vichy Government.

Father became very good at forging documents because he was meticulous and his handwriting was superb. Forging documents required not only talent, but also courage, for if Father had been caught, he would have been tortured and shot. Yet, he went ahead with his forging activities, seemingly without hesitations. His wish to resist the Vichy Government came more from inner feelings that owed nothing to any Jewish ancestry.

Change of identities among Frenchmen became so common later that the German police started to check on the real identity of anyone they arrested by looking up true birth certificates in the city halls where the arrested person said he or she was born. It became impossible, therefore, to make up identities of imaginary people. One way to overcome this problem was to give identities of real people. This meant that during the last two years of the German occupation of France there were sometimes two individuals with the same identity, obviously not in the same town, but miles apart. This presented quite a problem for those who had taken the identity of someone else. They had to know intimately the life of the person of whose name they borrowed. In other words, this could only work between friends. For example, my parents at the end of the war took the names of Gout. The real Gout couple were very good friends of our parents who hoped they knew enough about the Gouts to fool the police if they were arrested. Fortunately for our parents nothing happened to them during the last ten months of the German occupation when they were Mr.and Mrs. Gout. But, what bothered Mother during that time of her life was the fact that Madame Gout had been divorced, and Mother had a terrible time coping with the idea of divorce. And yet, if she were to be Madame Gout, she had to consider Father as her second husband, a feeling that was completely foreign to her. Well, I suppose that to save one's life one had to put up with this kind of thing.

In the case of Jews changes of identities were found to be a far more effective way to escape Nazi persecution than becoming members of the Catholic Church or a protestant denomination. Early in 1941 it was suggested to our parents by a family friend, who was protestant, that one way Gilles and I would be better off was to become protestant. She suggested a pastor whom she knew personally and who was interested in this endeavor. Father, the apostle of anticlericalism, did not think it was a great idea, but he did not oppose our having a meeting with the pastor. So Gilles and I went to see him. It was a perfect disaster, for the man had no understanding of our situation, did not answer our questions and proselytized for two hours with desperate energy. We left for home and told our parents about our catastrophic meeting. They never suggested a second meeting. In the long run whether we were protestant or not would have made no difference. The Nazis, French or German, never paid attention to a baptism certificate that could be easily forged. Furthermore, as the reader is aware, a Jew was a Jew was a Jew. No paper forged or not would change his or her "racial" origin. This type of resistance to Vichy decrees backfired.

If Gilles and I remained uncommitted to any of the religious faiths, there were others who lost their faith in their response to life threatening conditions, such as those in concentration camps. This was the case of a Polish friend of ours named Ruth. As a young Jewish girl she was arrested with her whole family and sent to Dachau. Her entire family was wiped out, but luckily she survived. When the concentration camp was liberated, she decided to accept the invitation of a French girl whom she had befriended in the camp, to go with her to France where her parents had a farm near Nancy. It took them two weeks to get there. A month later, after eating eggs, meat, and vegetables in abundance and drinking milk their young bodies were back to normal. Then, turning their minds to something more exciting than eating they decided to go dancing. At the dance, our friend met a young American soldier whom she married within a month. She was brought back to the United States as a war bride. Her husband, David, was a practicing Jew. She let him and her two children go to the synagogue, but she never went with them. After her experience in Dachau, she had lost faith in God. "If there were a God," she explained to me, "he could not have permitted the holocaust." To forget it and to be able to live a normal life –and she did– she had the concentration camp number that had been tattooed on her arm removed.

Chapter 14

Hope At Last

No American will think that it is wrong of me if I proclaim that to have the United States at our side was to me the greatest joy.
WINSTON CHURCHILL

Between the June of 1940 and June of the following year hope for the liberation of France was dim. The only nation fighting Germany was England and its commonwealth. Though the British had been able to prevent the Germans from invading England, they were losing every other battle. However, the fate of Europe was going to change.

June 22 was Father's birthday and in 1941, as a birthday present, Hitler gave him hope. He invaded the Soviet Union. We heard the news while we were cutting roses in the greenhouses. I still remember Father saying: " This is the biggest mistake Hitler could make, for if he cannot destroy the Russian armies before the winter, he will lose the war. No invading army has ever overcome the Russian winter. I believe that like Napoleon, he is going to his grave." Prophetic words. The only worry that Father had during that day was that Winston Churchill, a well known anti-communist, might make peace with Hitler in order to crush communism. Fortunately, that very night Churchill reassured us. He made the announcement that he was going to help Stalin. That day, for the first time, we saw a small light at the end of the proverbial tunnel.

Father's prediction came true. The Germans went very far into Russian territory but had to stop a few miles from Moscow because winter had set in. Their armored divisions got stuck in a sea of mud. Hitler suffered his first defeat. He lost men and material, and though he was able to go as far as the Volga the following year and fight the Soviet Army for another three years, he finally lost the war.

The next break for us Europeans came on December 7, 1941. Pearl Harbor (we had to look it up on the map to find out where it was located) was attacked. Again we worried. Would the Americans declare war on Japan, but not on Germany? Again, we were relieved. The U.S. Congress declared war on both countries. Our fear was also unfounded because Germany and Italy declared war on the United States December 11, 1941 in fulfillment of their treaty with Japan. Now we could see in the tunnel the light getting stronger: the Germans would be defeated. What we needed was patience, a lot of it.

Things were rough but we managed- We were fed and Gilles and I were busy getting an education at the local high school. But I wanted to do something more useful to help the defeat of the Axis. I had just turned 17 and I thought of joining the Allied Forces. But how? I asked my high school friend Alain Cianfanelli to help me out. He thought that my dream could materialize. He told me that he would contact a captain in the Wermarcht—who was really a British agent. The captain was to be picked up with other members of the British Intelligence in a submarine off the French Riviera near the town of Cavalaire where my parents passed so many wonderful days in 1916. In a few days they would be on British soil. If I could be there at the right time, I might join these men. Alain told me that he would let me know the day of the meeting. I waited two weeks. Then came the bad news: the Captain had been betrayed, arrested and shot by the Gestapo when his real identity had been revealed. The deal was off. My dream of escaping from France and joining the Allied Forces remained a dream for quite a while.

In July I had to present myself for the first part of the baccalaureate. This is the exam all seniors in high school have to take in order to continue their studies at university level. The examinations cover all the subjects that students have taken during the last six years. They are generally hard and discriminating. The written examinations that lasted two days had to be taken at Cannes, only a few miles away from Antibes. To get there I rode my bicycle. Few of us students were really in the mood to take the exam. However, we did our best and waited for the verdict. Well, something happened. The officials discovered that there had been a leak and exam questions had been known in advance to many students. We were asked to take the exam again. So I went to Cannes a second time and failed the exam. But, fortunately, I had another chance in September. During the last part of the Summer I tackled the courses in which I was weak and I was successful in my second attempt to pass the written test. Now I had to pass the oral examination which was to be taken in Nice. My brother was so proud of me that the morning I took the train for Nice, he shined my shoes for the first and last time. I passed the exam with the equivalent of a B-. Things were looking up.

A few days later we were able to take a short vacation at Pralognan-La Vanoise, in the Alps. I remember little from my stay there except what happened to me when we took the train back to Antibes that summer. During the German occupation the only means of rapid locomotion from city to city was the railway. Ordinary French people could not drive their cars which had been taken by the German authorities or if they still had cars, there was no gasoline to use. Hence, walking or riding bicycles were the only means of getting from one place to another if the distance was not too great. Long trips had to be taken by trains which were always too full. No one could go to the toilets for they were permanently occupied by people who could not find any other place to sit or even stand. After our stay at Pralognan-La Vanoise, Mother, Gilles, and I attempted to take the train from Annecy, in Savoie, to go back to Antibes. Mother and Gilles managed to get into the overcrowded train which departed, but I was left stranded on the platform. As I was running next to the window of the compartment my family was in, two strong men put down the large window, bent over it, and caught me under the arm pits and pulled me in.

An important event in the life of every Frenchman occurred on November 11, 1942. That day American forces successfully landed in North Africa. Unfortunately, because the Vichy Government chose to fight the Allied troops and because the American High Command did not trust the Resistance in North Africa, fifteen hundred French lives and nearly the same number of British and American lives were lost. In response to the American landing, the Germans, abrogating the terms of the 1940 armistice, occupied all of France except eight departments that the Italians occupied (Haute Savoie, Savoie, Basses Alpes, Hautes Alpes, Isère, Drome, Alpes Maritimes, and Corsica).

For us it was a lucky break to be under direct Italian occupation, for compared to the Germans, Italians were generally decent human beings. As a matter of fact the Italian soldiers helped a lot of the local French population to survive, in particular the children, by feeding them rice and pasta out of their kitchens. A few Italian soldiers made a habit of coming onto our property to serenade the women who were putting roses in baskets for us. They asked us to listen to the BBC. to find out when the Americans were going to land in France so they could go home. They were the first to invent the slogan: "Make love, not war."

After the landing of Allied troops in Northern Africa, the attitude of the German Occupation authorities changed for the worse. They realized that there was a real possibility that they could lose the war. They became vicious towards the French underground, the Jews, and anyone they suspected of being their enemies. On the other hand, many Frenchmen who, up to that time had been collaborating with the Germans, switched sides. This was very evident with policemen who realized that they had played the wrong card. If France was to be liberated, they needed to show that they had helped the underground. And so they started to alert potential victims of a raid before the raid was executed; they facilitated the escape of Resistance fighters from prisons, and finally, they became themselves

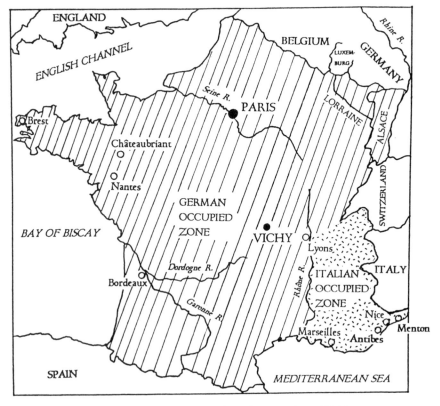

FRANCE—November 1942 - September 1943

part of the underground. There is no doubt that the French Resistance, which until November 1942 had been a small group of dedicated patriots grew stronger and stronger after the landing of Allied forces in North Africa. By the end of 1942 Resistance activities grew to a large number: gathering information, producing clandestine papers, forming embryonic military units, hiding Jews, Resisters and Allied Aviators on the run, manning escape routes out of France for them, producing false papers and ration cards, and establishing communications between underground networks and London.

On the other hand, November 1942 was an important date for Vichy. It could not play any more the double game that it had played so far. It chose to become an unequivocal partner with Hitler and lost forever what remained of its dignity. Many of its members, such as Pierre Laval, were to lose their heads.

Gilles, London 1939.

Five poilus, World War I. I think Father is on the right.

Clair Matin: The long Grape Arbor.

Clair Matin: The Patio.

Mother in the Library of Clair Matin.

Menton-Garavan: The Harbor.

*Antibes, December 1940. Father and the two boys.
Alain on the right.*

*Antibes, December 1940. From left to right: Alain,
Aunt Alice, Mother, Gilles, and Father.*

Antibes, December 1940. Uncle Fernand, Gilles, and Alain.

Skiers at Monêtier, 1943. From left to right: Alain, Michel, Gilbert, and Gilles.

Robert Rousset is on the far right.

Llivia, a rocky, waterless part of the plateau of Las Puntas.

PART 6

SURVIVAL IN OCCUPIED FRANCE

Chapter 15

Boarders At Briançon High School

Valleys that descend to abysses, Mountains that touch the sky.
VAUBAN, DESCRIBING THE SITE OF BRIANÇON

Though we were better off under Italian occupation than under German occupation, Father soon realized that it was not safe any more to be in Antibes. His name was on the list of those who were the enemies of Mussolini and chances were that sooner or later he would be arrested. He decided that we should all leave the French Riviera and find another place where we would be safe. Our parents thought of the town of Briançon in the Alps to which their friends, the Bouverots, had just moved and where Mr. Bouverot now was the athletic coach at the local high school, the same position that he had at Menton.

Our parents decided that we, the children, Gilles, our cousin Francis, and I would be safe as high school boarders in Briançon because we were not known in the region and Mr. Bouverot would keep an eye on us. We found out later that Mr. Bouverot was very active in the underground. He was to play an important part in 1944 as a member of the Committee of Liberation of Briançon, the political entity that would govern the town for a few months after it was liberated.

Before we left Antibes Father asked me to help him bury a few U.S. dollar bills that he had and that he could not deposit in a bank, for they would have been confiscated by the Vichy Government. Father put all his dollar bills in coffee cans. Then, after making sure that no one was watching us, he put the cans at the bottom of a large hole that he had made me dig in the cemented patio in the back of the house. Though he had never done any masonry in his life, he covered the hole with cement so well that no one could imagine that the patio had been recently disturbed. I never knew how much money Father buried that day. All he told me was that if one of us came out alive after the liberation of France, he had better not forget the location of the cache. Father came back two years later and retrieved his money.

On November 13, Gilles, Francis and I put a few things in the baskets of our bicycles and were off bicycling up and down the Alps to reach the town of Briançon which was then under Italian occupation. This was not the first time we would be separated from our parents. After all, we had passed five months in England all by ourselves. But this time we did not know how long we would be separated or the conditions of such a separation. However, we were mature enough to realize that this was the best solution under the circumstances.

We had bicycled all our lives, but we never made such a long trip as the one we had planned. It was not so much the distance of 100 miles that we would travel as the difficulty of climbing over four mountain passes each at least 3000 feet high. Our bicycles were not new, but they were very adequate for they had balloon tires and derailleurs that would enable us to travel across the Alps. We took off early in the morning on the first leg of the trip. This was to reach Grasse by the back roads. Grasse is one the best well known and most wealthy towns in France, for it is the capital of the perfume industry. It is surrounded by a sea of flowers, consisting mainly of roses and jasmine. Most of these flowers are sent to the sixty factories in town, where the flower oils are distilled. Sometimes the factories do not have enough flowers and are forced to buy them from other parts of the French Riviera. This is what happened in the summer of 1942. Gilles and I collected rose petals by the bag full off the rose bushes in our greenhouses. Roses bloomed so profusely in the summer that no one bought roses from June to August. We sent those bags to Grasse. But selling rose petals by the pound did not make us rich. We learned that summer that if there was money in the perfume industry, it was not for those who harvest flowers. All our summer efforts netted us no more than 50 francs or 10 U.S. dollars.

We went through Grasse in a hurry, for we had no time to visit the perfume factories and see if we could differentiate the 6,000 perfume fragrances. We continued our trip towards the town of Castellane, following the Route Napoléon, so called because it is the one that Napoléon Bonaparte took when, in 1815, he came back from exile on the island of Elba. Going through the Alps he reached Paris. People then rallied to him and once more he was fighting all Europe.

I am sure that Napoléon had it smoother than we, for our mountain cycling was very rough. The road leaving Grasse was climbing fast, for

Grasse is at about 100 feet above sea level and the first pass we came to, the Col du Pilon, reaches 2400 feet. We wondered if we were training ourselves for the Tour de France. Well, not really, for we stopped frequently to drink and rest. After this first pass, we went down for a while, but soon after we had to climb again towards the second pass, the col de Valferriere, at an altitude of 3200 feet. Again we found the down hill from that pass refreshing. Then, we had to climb even harder to reach the third pass, Le col de Luens, at an altitude of 3000 feet. From there we coasted down to Castellane.

The worst was to come. We had to climb our last and highest mountain pass, le Col de Leques, at 3500 feet. As we climbed the very steep road, with innumerable hairpins, we started to have serious body pains. Pushing on the pedals became harder and harder. Our rear ends rubbing hard on the bicycle seats became raw. Then it happened: Francis'bicycle broke down. The two pedals which generally are at an angle of 180 degrees from each other were now at an angle of 135 degrees, which made pedaling very hard to do. Francis was not as athletic as we were. He hated to walk, and when I asked him why he had two feet, he used to answer, "to climb on the bus." Gilles decided to switch bicycles with him. Fortunately for all of us there were only a few miles more to reach the pass and we were soon going down reaching the important town of Digne without any more incidents.

We had gone through one of the most spectacular mountain roads of France, but we had not been able to enjoy its beauty. We were now very tired and ready to finish the trip in better comfort. There were no trains between Antibes and Digne, but there were trains from Digne to Briançon and we decided that we would end our trip by using this mean of locomotion. Without any problem, we arrived at Briançon which is the terminal railway station at the end of the Durance Valley, right at the confluence of the Durance and the Guisane rivers.

The region of Briançon was already inhabited 3000 years ago as evidenced by the discovery of many neolitic artifacts. It has always been important from a military and economic point of view. Briançon (under the name of Brigantum) was an important Roman city. A possible reason for its past and present prominence is that the town, being at the intersection of five valleys, has always been a thoroughfare between France and Italy. Briançon is now a gracefully picturesque, merchant, industrial, and tourist town, which is believed to be the highest in Europe as it stands at an altitude of 4,347 feet. Though it has not too many inhabitants Briançon is very important politically for the town is the sous-prefecture of the Department of the Hautes Alpes.

Briançon is blessed by a fantastic climate. Lots of sun and a moderate rainfall. Before World War II it was a haven for patients with tuberculosis. Many of them recovered after passing a few months in a sanatorium. A few of these sanatoria were perched on the top of the hill overhanging the old town. Now that tuberculosis is no longer the scourge as it once was, the town has become a haven for those who are affected with allergies.

Like many French towns, Briançon is made of two distinctive parts, the old and the new. The old one, walled in, is perched on the top of a hill. It was enclosed by ramparts after it had been put to the torch in the 16th century. Forts built in the first part of the 18th century by Vauban, the military architect, are perched on the summits around the Old Town and were still in use during World War II. A triple line of walls surrounds the town which can be entered by a drawbridge at the bottom of the hill, or by a massive door at the top of the hill. No car is allowed through the very narrow and very steep streets. Only delivery trucks are permitted to deliver their cargo. The main street runs straight down hill with numerous mule-steps on each side. It is called La Grande Gargouille, because in the middle of the street there is a water gutter (Gargouille) through which water runs like a torrent carrying away refuse. On the sides of the Grande Gargouille are small stores ranging from bakeries, bookstores, and gift shops, to sporting good stores. Most of the houses in that part of the city date from the Middle Ages. Half way up La Grande Gargouille there is a fountain dating back from 1215 A.D.

On the west side and at the base of the old town is the new town. A main avenue going steeply down links the old Town up the hill to the commercial district, at the bottom of the hill, with the most important stores, the banks, the Railway Station, and factories. On both sides of the main avenue, nested in the hill, are numerous homes. On the right side, halfway down, stands the Lycée (High School). This high school at Briançon was a school for boys only. I have no idea where the high school for girls was. However, the last year (roughly a year beyond the senior year in an American High School), both girls and boys were attending the same required classes of philosophy and mathematics. The reason for this unusual mixture of sexes was that many students flunked the examinations of the first part of the baccalaureate and there would have been, in as small town as Briançon, too few male and female students in the advanced classes if they had been separated in two different schools. So for the first time in our lives we had girls in our class. What a change the way we looked at things! A few romances flourished, but nothing serious could have ever developed from this, for the immediate future was too bleak. A few of these students, male and female, were to fight the Germans a few months later and some died during the fighting.

Briançon, as we mentioned, was then under the Italian occupation and therefore we were relatively safe there. However, we had to be cautious in expressing our political opinions. One reason, among others, was that we could not entirely trust the High School principal. Our mistrust was amply justified, for later, he betrayed some students who were working for the underground. Because of this, he was arrested during the liberation of the town and passed a few months in jail.

Our life as boarders at the high school was hard. We did not have enough food to eat. The daily diet was cooked cabbages, turnips, and rutabagas, hardly the right one for growing boys. From time to time there was what the cook aristocratically called a stew in which a few precious pieces of meat were swimming with a few boiled potatoes and carrots. These pieces of meat had to be distributed equally among the twenty boarders who were sitting around a large table. Equally is, of course, a very difficult word to understand under these circumstances. We understood it to mean that each one of us had to have the same number of pieces of meat. But there are pieces of meat and pieces of meat. Not every piece has the same volume and the same weight. Two of the big boys were in charge of the distribution. One would say: "For whom is this piece?" The other who did not see the meat morsel would announce the name of one of the boys around the table and that boy would get the piece of meat. On the surface this seemed to be fair. However, in reality, the first big boy who asked the question would kick under the table the foot of the second boy if the piece of meat was big, but would not do it if the piece was small. So the big boys, among whom were my brother and myself, were always favored. In spite of this obvious favoritism we were always hungry. To forget about the constant hunger pains I used to get involved in the most complex mathematics problems that I could find.

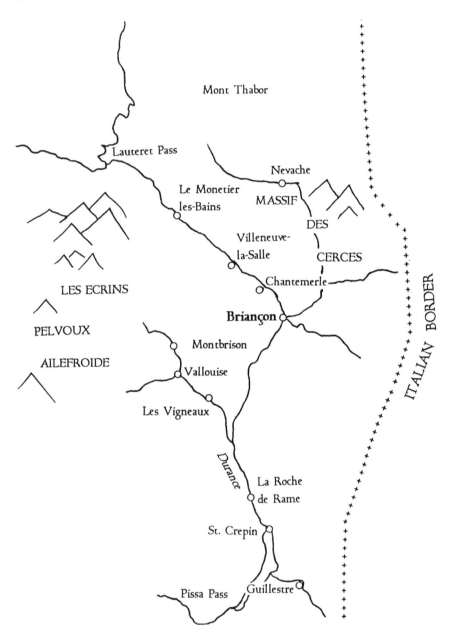

Briançon and surroundings

Things improved just a little for me personally in June 1943. As I turned 18 years old I was given a tobacco card by the government. This permitted me to buy two packs of French cigarettes, the famous gauloises, every ten days. Since I did not smoke, I exchanged these cigarettes for food with some of my schoolmates who had access to sources of food, because their parents had farms around Briançon. One day I made the bargain of a lifetime. I exchanged one cigarette for one egg, two walnuts, and a piece of ham.

This exchange of cigarettes for food was great for me. But for the real smokers the war years were a nightmare. They were saving cigarette butts and smoking them. They had figured out that if they took the tobacco of three cigarette butts and wrapped it in a thin cigarette paper they could make one cigarette. Based on this fact, our mathematics instructor asked us one day the following problem: "How many cigarettes can one make out of 10 cigarette butts?", The mathematical answer is 4 cigarettes and two butts are left over. But there is a catch which leads to the following very important answer for a true-smoker:

Out of nine butts, he can make three cigarettes which he smokes. Now he has three butts, out of which he makes one cigarette. After smoking it he has one butt, to which he adds the tenth butt. He borrows one butt from a friend, makes a cigarette and after smoking it he gives back the resulting newly created butt to his friend.

Another thing that helped me physically during these troubled times has to do with vitamins, many of which we lacked during the occupation. One was vitamin D. This vitamin, which is essential for the absorption of calcium in the bones, is called the sunshine vitamin, because it is synthesized in the skin by the rays of the sun. However, in the winter, when there is little sunshine, little vitamin D is synthesized in the skin. When I was a child, Mother, like many other mothers, gave Gilles and me, or rather attempted to give us, cod liver oil, which was at the time the best source of Vitamin D. She found one day a large bottle of cod liver oil and gave it to me because I was an exceptional child who loved the taste of cod liver oil. So during my stay at Briançon I gave myself a large spoonful of cod liver oil every three days. I never developed any of the symptoms of vitamin D deficiency.

Chapter 16

Le Monêtier les Bains, a small heaven

My life has crept so long on a broken wing thro's cells of madness, haunts of horror and fear, that I came to be grateful at last for a little thing.
ALFRED LORD TENNYSON

A week after we arrived in Briançon our parents came there, not by bicycles, but by train taking the long way from Antibes to Marseilles, to Valence and at last to Briançon. They had left the management of their property in the hands of their friends, Mr. and Mrs. Gout. After the liberation they were able to get it back and sell it to the same man who sold it to them four years before, Mr. Tourdre, who then sold it again making a large profit after having divided it into two lots.

Our parents found a hiding place in a small village near Briançon called "Le Monêtier les Bains", deep inside the valley of La Guisane which was free of Italian soldiers and police. This village, at an altitude of 5,000 feet, remains in our memory as a small island of heaven in the sea of hell. Many of its inhabitants played an important role in the resistance against the Germans and helped many political refugees to escape Nazi and Vichy persecution. Among the resisters was Mr. Robert, the owner of the hotel, in which our parents stayed for quite a while. The hotel, now modernized, is still managed by the same family.

The village of Le Monêtier slopes down to the river, La Guisane, which has carved out the valley of the same name. The river has its source to the north, at the Lauteret pass, 6200 feet high up in the Alps and ends in the Durance just past Briançon. The Lauteret pass takes its name from a small temple (Altaretum) that the Romans built at its top. The U-shaped valley of the Guisane consists of a charming pastoral landscape with meadows and background of towering mountains. This beautiful valley is far greener than the Romanche valley north of the Lauteret pass. And yet the climate of the region is very dry, with a blue sky that is reminiscent of the one in Provence. The Chamber of Commerce of Briançon claims that there are 300 days of sunshine in that city. The amount of snow that falls in the region during the

winter months varies considerably from year to year. In the 1940's when
Gilles and I were in the Briançonnais there was little snow, though enough
to ski, and certainly enough of it on the top of the mountains to feed the
rivers keeping the vegetation green during the summer.

Immediately north of Le Monêtier the ascent to the Col du Lauteret
begins in earnest. A long, rising road, followed by a series of wide turns
through a grazing country gives place to more forbidding scenery as the
gradient increases. Near the top there is a tunnel protecting the road from
landslides. Beyond this the southern approach to another pass, the Col du
Galibier, appears on the right, with the ribbon-like road winding up the
giant slopes of the mountain.

A few hundred feet from the pass one can see the entrance of a tunnel
passing into the mountain. This tunnel is no ordinary tunnel. It is about half
a mile long but does not lead anywhere. It was never finished, and during
the Italian and German occupation it became the headquarters of the local
F.F.I. (French Forces of the Interior). From time to time between November
1942 and September 1944, the Italian troops and the German troops who
replaced them after September 1943 came up the Guisane Valley. But the
F.F.I. were always alerted of their coming by patriotic telephone operators
and they would withdraw higher up in the mountains and go back into their
tunnel when the troops had left. From time to time, especially during the
winter months when the snow was abundant and when only skiers could
move, many of the F.F.I. went down the valley to see their loved ones. It was
on one of these occasions that Father was able to talk to a handsome and
friendly twenty year old guerrilla. During the conversation the young man
told him of his feelings when, for the first time, he shot a German soldier.
It had been a very hard decision for him to make. But, when he realized
what the German soldier might do to him and his friends, he found out he
had no choice but to fire his gun. After that he had no qualms about shooting other German soldiers. Months later he and his friends with the help of
Americans and the First French Army were going to liberate Briançon.

Going down from the Lauteret pass to Briançon, one can see on the left
of the valley, the dolomite mountains of Le Galibier, Les Cerces, La
Ponsonniere, and l'Aiguille du Lauzet, a sharp needle pointing into the
blue sky. Further south, the mountains are not so rugged, but still as high.
It is in these mountains that coal was found as early as the sixteenth century. But the coal is of such poor quality that before the war the mines were

closed. It comes in powder form and has to be wetted and fashioned into large cakes that can be carried easily. It contains so much sand or clay that fifty percent of it has to be thrown out after it is burned. However, during World War II the mines were reopened because there was such a scarcity of fuel that the people of the region were happy to burn this type of coal which kept their houses very warm during the extremely cold months. Throughout the occupation, the mines had a lot of workers on the payroll. However, many of these workers were not miners at all, but members of the underground forces who needed an official home and working papers so they would not attract the attention of the Italian or German authorities.

On the right of the valley, one can see against the blue sky the Oisans-Pelvoux, the well known chain of peaks and glaciers. The highest peak is Le Pic des Agneaux which reaches 11,500 feet. It looks like a black diamond in a lake of ice that overflows in the valley of the Casset. On the right of the glacier there is a high wall of bluish rocks that is crowned with shining snow. This is the Dome of Le Monêtier which stands to about 9400 feet with its own glacier in the small valley of Tabuc. South of the dome to the end of the valley, the mountains are not as high and are made of limestone instead of granite. There is a pass across these mountains called L'Eychauda, that played an important role during the liberation of Southern France. Through it Allied agents, who had been parachuted further south, went north in early August 1944 to prepare the route of the invasion that was to occur on the 15th of that month.

I would ike to explain why Le Monêtier became a heaven for Gilles and me and why we were anxious to come every week-end to be fed. We had found that Madame Robert, wife of the owner of the hotel where our parents were then hiding, cooked some fantastic meals. My saliva is still flowing freely in my mouth when I think of her "Gratin dauphinois" in which pieces of ham, mind you, and lots of cheese were lost in a sea of buttered potatoes. In some way Madame Robert's cooking was the reason that we did not lose our health during those dark days. After eating her meals we could put up with the miserable food that confronted us during the week days at the High School. Later in the same village our parents managed to have in an old stone house, a basement apartment which was dark and dirty, but warm, with a stove where our mother could cook and feed us comfortably during week-ends.

It is seven miles from Briançon to Le Monêtier. This trip did not present any problem in the late spring, summer, and early fall. It was easy for us to go by bicycle. However, during the hard and cold winter months we had to take the local bus which ran on wood gas instead of gasoline. In this very energy inefficient system, green wood was burnt in a twenty gallon metal boiler strapped to the fender. The combustion products were fed directly into the carburetor. The "gazogene"bus, as it was called, was sometimes so crowded that the young passengers, like us, had to ride on the roof with chickens in cages, luggage and boxes of all kinds. Many times we found it easier to ski the whole way. I remember a particular time when we did ski to the village through a violent snow storm. We arrived at Le Monêtier frozen, and starved as usual. Our parents were not there that week end, but had left us a few groceries in their tiny apartment. It was the first time that we had to cook for ourselves. Our supper, I still remember, was oatmeal and fried potatoes, not French fried, but American fried. The food was good and we survived.

Later we became better cooks but were always on the lookout for food. And so we were very happy to learn from the local people that there were no poisonous mushrooms in the region. In the summer of 1943, again when our parents were away from their small apartment, Gilles and I decided to hike in the mountains and pick mushrooms. We found this to be an easy task, for after three hours we had twenty four pounds of fresh mushrooms in our knapsacks. Then, after getting advice from the baker's wife, we cooked them with olive oil in a pan over a low fire. It took a long time, for mushrooms have a tremendous amount of water. We finally got about two pounds of fried mushrooms and we ate them in one meal.

Our parents loved to hike and they passed happy hours on the many trails that have been carved off the slopes of the mountains that surround Le Monêtier. When we were staying with them we usually accompanied them. However, since they were quite a few years older than we were, it was not unusual for them to stop to rest. But Gilles and I were full of energy and we had to spend it one way or another. We climbed rocks or pole-vaulted across the torrents near by. Our poles were simply tree branches that we had barked off and cleaned. We never became experts, but we had a lot of fun jumping, though sometimes we landed in the water. Was this part of the fun? Yes, of course. Being in the mountains was very appeasing for the four of us. It calmed our fears that the future might be far worse than the present.

Chapter 17

Skiing in the Alps

THE SKI RUNNER
Above you burns a molten-copper sun,
Before you hangs the imminent abyss,
Flaring in white,-a desperate game to run,
This frozen speedway to the deeps of Dis!
Now bend your heart and foot and spirit straight,
that none may shrink,
Then down, down the eagle takes his flight!
Sailing an instant on the wings of Fate,
An aeon poising on the utter brink,-
Then out! into a wilderness of light!

AUTHOR UNKNOWN.

Because of its location in the High Alps, Briançon and its surroundings were already a center for skiing in the 1940's. This was great for us who had been skiing since we were six and five years old respectively. At Serres Chevalier, a few miles from Briançon, there was a ski lift used for training by the French Olympic ski team which, after adopting Emile Allais's skiing method, was the best in the world. After earning a bronze medal in the 1936 Winter Olympics, Allais had become the world champion of downhill skiing in 1937. At that time the top speed was 45 miles an hour, now it is more than 100.

Gilles and I were good skiers, but some of our schoolmates at Briançon were excellent ones and possible future members of the national skiing team. As a matter of fact, two of them, a young man and a young woman, did become members. Unfortunately, the young man lost a leg fighting the Germans in 1944. An arrangement had been made between the high school and the ski lift officials that permitted us to use the teleferic free of charge. However there was the following stipulation: we had to use the same gondola as the members of the team were using. This meant that since they went down the slope in not more than four minutes and since each gondola was going up every 15 minutes, we, the hope of

France, had to go down in less than 10 minutes to have time to take it. Though this required for some of us a lot of efforts, we generally managed to do this and had a lot of fun at it. Years later Gilles and I could be distinguished from other skiers from far away by the way we slalomed, jumping like tigers on the front ends of our skis just like Emile Allais used to do.

However, what we liked the best was mountain skiing. Climbing in the virgin snow through the forest, looking at animals which were not afraid of us, hearing only the sounds of nature, and forgetting the war, was pure joy. I particularly remember a climb my brother, a friend of ours, and I made in the winter of 1943. A skiing party of three is ideal. It has been suggested that skiing alone is very enjoyable because one is forever proposing obstacles to oneself and then setting forth to surmount them. In skiing the obstacles may be distance or altitude, daring speed or skillful turns which a certain course requires. In conquering these obstacles, attention is diverted from the lack of companionship. However, I believe that skiing alone is foolhardy. for one can fall, get hurt, and remain lying motionless on a slope for hours taking the risk of not being rescued. I realized this once when I went down a mountain and found myself airborne for more than fifty feet, landing very close to a tree. Nothing happened to me, but I could have been hurt and no one would have known where I was. A two member party is not much better than a one member party, because if one sustains an injury, too much responsibility is thrown upon the other. But if there are three, two always are at hand to aid the other. However, parties of more than three are generally unwieldy. So Gilles and I went to look for our high school friend who lived with his mother and his grandfather in a small village, called Le Casset, two miles north from Le Monêtier. His father was a war prisoner in Germany. The Casset is a very picturesque village with its fields full of daffodils in June and its 17th Century very high steepled church. When one is inside the church, one can hear the perpetual murmur of the Guisane River close by.

That particular winter there was a lot of snow in the valley and in the mountains. The three of us decided to climb the mountain in the back of the village. In the 1940's mountain climbing was not only a sport, but also an adventure. We used to ski with no fancy clothes and our skis were rather primitive. The only important part of the equipment was a good pair of mountain shoes. To help us climb mountains we had seal skins.

The hair of the seal skins gripped the snow and prevented us from slipping backwards. This permitted us to climb slopes of up to a 25 degree angle.

As we reached the first slopes, the sun had begun to temper the biting cold, warming our skin, our blood and the air in our lungs. Ten minutes later, we shed our wind-proof jackets. The climbing of this particular mountain took us four hours. We enjoyed every minute of them. The trees, heavily draped with icy snow, commenced to get smaller. At last we left the last thin line of evergreen shrubs behind and emerged on the open slopes of snow. We stopped for a few minutes and looked down the valley which seemed so far away with the river now only a dark winding line and the village a collection of toy houses. Pretty as it was we were impatient to reach the top, anticipating our descent, a few moments of pure delight during which we would demonstrate our skill of turning right or left as occasion would demand, or jumping or coming to a standstill if that be best.

However, when we came to the top, a storm was brewing in the East. We thought it was prudent to go down immediately. We expected to do this in a matter of half an hour or less. It took us far longer. After a few turns I broke the tip of one of my skis. Unfortunately for me, plastic tips that one can now slide on broken skis had not been invented yet, and the only thing I could do was to go down on one ski. This, of course, retarded us considerably. Gilles and our friend cussed me profusely, for they had to wait for me during our descent. Fortunately, we reached Le Casset before the blinding storm struck us although the snow was falling heavily by then.

Our friend's mother wanted Gilles and me to dry off and warm up before we made the last leg of our trip, so she invited us into her home. This was an old house. On the first floor, sheep, cows, chickens and cats were sharing space with the grandfather who had a bed in the corner. The ceiling had an opening so that the heat of these animals could rise and keep the rest of the house warm. There will be no comment on the smell that permeated throughout the house. Our friend and his mother lived on the second floor. We went up and sat close to the fireplace where large pine logs were burning. After a fifteen minutes break we decided to go back to Le Monêtier. The storm was now very bad and our friend's mother gave us a small glass of moonshine. This was my first and last glass of moonshine in my life. Its alcohol warmed our bodies giving us the energy to run, and within twenty minutes we reached our parents'temporary home. There, we immediately collapsed in a heap in our common bed due to the dual effects of fatigue and the brew.

While we were at Briançon, we not only became good skiers but also mountain climbers. We had climbed mountains before the war especially in Switzerland. But we got excellent lessons from a superb athlete, Mr. Rousset, who was our gymnastics instructor at the high school. Like Mr. Bouverot, our gymnastic coach and friend, he was a member of the underground, an officer in the Secret Army which was to play an important role in liberating the region in August 1944. He also played an important role in guiding the Italian soldiers across the Alps back to Italy when the Italian army surrendered to the Allies in 1943. Our experience in the mountains was going to pay off in our escape from France later in 1944.

Chapter 18

Resistance Stories

A special agent in London was told that he would be dropped closed to a French village, that he was to pick up a bicycle that would be waiting for him next to the Church wall and go to the next village to meet a friend. Everything went allright until he jumped out of the plane and found that his parachute was not opening. "Oh, my God," he said, "The next bad thing that is going to happen to me will be that I am not going to find the bicycle."

HUMOR IN THE RESISTANCE.

It was impossible to predict what people would do during the war years. Shy people became heroes; extroverted people would hide. I remember the case of one particular young man-Ginet was his name- whom our family knew. As a young child he was scared of the dark and needed a light in his room before he could fall asleep. Now, in 1943, at the age of twenty two he was part of the underground. During these war years important people were picked up out of France either by small planes that landed during the night or by submarines that also at night approached very close to the rocky French Riviera. In both cases the only way the pilot of the plane or the captain of the submarine could see the location of their landing was if some underground agents by using flashlights indicated the exact position. One of these agents was our young friend. Here he was now in the darkest possible night signaling a submarine crew where to land, taking the chance of being shot on the spot. The little shy boy Ginet had grown into a very courageous young man.

Because the behavior of men and women was impossible to predict during these years of war and suffering it was often necessary to make a prompt judgment as to who could be your friend. How did you judge? Was it by looking into someone's eyes? There are abundant stories from that period that demonstrate that indeed people could be trusted and act humanely and even be asked to do things that they would never do ordinarily. One of the most striking is a story of what happened to my own mother. One day, in the fall of 1943, Mother was returning by train from

Antibes to Briançon having attended to some family business. The door
of her railway compartment was closed. As usual most people were
asleep, Others were reading. The door opened and a man about thirty
years old saw my mother and, without saying a word, deposited on her lap
a two year old child. Mother immediately knew what was going on and
did not say a word either. She knew what she had to do. The father had
trusted her and the message to her was clear: "If I do not come back, take
care of my child. He will be safe with you." Mother did take care of the
child wondering whether the child's father was going to be back or if he
was going to be arrested and would never show up again. In that case was
she supposed to raise that child? Fortunately for Mother, the young man
came back one hour later and said to Mother only two words, "thank
you," and disappeared with the child. Mother never saw them again. She
kept wondering whether or not she would have done the same with her
own child and how much courage this man had. She concluded that she
would have done the same.

A few weeks later, coming back again from Antibes, in the same train,
Mother sat next to a Wermacht Captain who was very polite and gentle-
manly. Mother spoke German and soon was conversing with him. The
subject soon switched from the weather to the war. It became apparent
that the Captain was very tired of the war and wanted to go home. It was
a real eye-opener for Mother that the morale in the German Army was not
as high as Hitler had made us believe. By the time they reached Briançon
Mother and the Captain had become friends. Together they entered the
railway station, the Captain carrying Mother's suitcase. They by-passed
the Gestapo checkpoint to the intense relief of Mother. I cannot remember what was in the suitcase, but there was something that she did not
want the Germans to see. Mother's adventure was not unique. The underground used old women to carry suitcases in which documents, radios or
even guns had been placed. One day a sixty-year old woman, the grand-
motherly type, was in a train with such a suitcase which was rather heavy.
During her trip she had befriended a teenager who seemed to be strong
enough to carry the suitcase. When she reached her destination she asked
him to do that. In exchange she would carry his small suitcase. He accepted and both went through the police checkpoint relieved that their suitcases had not been opened. When they were a few hundred yards from the
railway station the Grandmother thanked the young man for carrying the

suitcase and told him that he had carried a small submachine gun. The young man answered: "I understand Madame. As to you, you were carrying maps on which all the German gun emplacements and position of troops have been indicated !"

Chapter 19

Things Are Getting Worse
Time To Escape

When a building is about to fall down, all the mice desert it.

PLINY THE ELDER

In September 1943 I had to go back to Antibes to attempt the second part of the baccalaureate. If successful I would be able to enter the University. I had to go to Antibes, because my dossier was still in the hands of the administration on the French Riviera, which by that time was no longer occupied by the Italian troops, but by the German troops. During the summer of that year Italy had undergone internal upheaval brought about by the Allied invasion of Sicily. Italy was able to shake off the fascist yoke and Mussolini was replaced by Marshal Pietro Badoglio who put the former dictator under arrest. Two months later Italy surrendered to the Allies. It seems that army marshals, be they French or Italian, have a knack for surrendering. Unfortunately for the Allies, the Germans were prepared for this eventuality. With great dispatch they rescued Mussolini and occupied Italy as far south as Rome. Unfortunately for us, they also poured into the Italian-held territory in Southeastern France. From now on the lot of the Resisters and the Jews was to become worse, far worse.

Unknown to us, Mussolini had shielded Italian Jews from the wrath of Hitler and had also extended his protection to the Jews, be they Italian, French, or stateless, in the eight departments of Southern France that they occupied. The Italian Foreign Ministry devised scheme after scheme to thwart and delay the French and German Nazi demands for their intended victims. This situation lasted until the fall of Mussolini. Now, without Italian protection they were going to be deported. Thousands of them were picked up in Nice and sent to concentration camps. Some were able to follow the Italian soldiers back to Italy through the Alps but got no further than the small villages in Northern Italy. There, hungry and exhausted from the long march, they were rounded up by the rapidly advancing

German Army and shipped to the death camps.

Knowing little about this new development, I went by train to Antibes and reached the town safely. There I rang the bell of the home of Monsieur and Madame Cordier who had been friends of my parents since World War I. It was perfectly safe for me to stay at their home for the few days in which I was going to attempt to pass the second part of the baccalaureate. I looked up my friend, Alain Cianfanelli, who also offered me lodging.

He told me that during that summer he had been arrested, but had managed to escape as he was led with others through the Nice railway station. He took advantage of a large influx of passengers to turn to the right instead of left as the other fifty prisoners did. Though he was very tall, the German guards did not see him leaving the pack and he lost himself in the crowd.

I borrowed a bicycle from him and rode it to Cannes two days in a row, just as I had done a year before. On the road to Cannes two black citroen cars passed me. I shuddered for these were the famous Gestapo cars, the first I ever saw. A few minutes later, as I was in front of the Carlton Hotel, I saw the cars again and the S.S. officers discussing on the sidewalk. Having been so far only under the Italian occupation I had no occasion of seeing any member of the dreadful Gestapo. This was my chance. In the streets were young German soldiers goosestepping, singing at the top of their lungs in anticipation of having a good time on the sandy beaches, swimming and frolicking in the warm water of the bay. They hoped to forget the real possibility of being killed on the Russian battlefront in the next few weeks. Looking at the members of the "master race" I became truly scared and I pedaled as fast as I could to the High School where a few minutes later I had the chance to write answers to thrilling questions in science, mathematics and philosophy.

A few days later I learned that I had flunked the examinations. This was predictable for my mind had not been exactly on passing the baccalaureate with flying colors, but rather how to survive in the most hellish environment in which one can find oneself. The next day I took the train back to Briançon and the bus to Le Monêtier. I had only one thought on my mind: Shall I join the Forces of the Underground or shall I escape from France and join the Allied Forces. I decided to go back to Briançon High School to stay in the math and science class for another year. Gilles who had sat successfully for the first part of the baccalaureate would take the same classes that I was repeating. As to Francis, who now had his high school degree, he had gone to the Lycée Champollion at Grenoble, an important industrial city in the Alps, north of Briançon. There he was to follow special courses to prepare himself to enter "L'Ecole Supérieure d'Electricité", one of the Grandes Ecoles de France. What was the nature of these national schools?

Though higher education in France is offered chiefly in the universities, a relatively small number of selected students receive their higher education in small specialized national schools, called the Grandes Ecoles, often attached to departments of governments, which train executives and specialists primarily for these departments. Admission to these schools is by highly competitive examination. Francis had always wanted to be an electrical engineer and had shown an aptitude for this since an early age. Now it was his chance to fulfill his dream. But, as he told us later the political and emotional environment in October 1943 when he went to Grenoble, was unbearable. Francis could not concentrate on his studies. He was terribly distressed about the fate of his mother who had been arrested a month before. He was separated from his adoptive parents (my own parents) and his adoptive brothers (Gilles and me). He was in constant fear of being arrested and executed as some of his friends were.

In late 1943, the Germans in Grenoble became raving mad after their barracks had been blown up. Looking for new quarters, they took revenge on the students physically kicking them out of their dormitories with rifle butts. Francis took refuge in Lyon among some of our cousins and continued his studies by correspondence. Yet, in spite of this hell on earth, he managed to get admittance later to L'Ecole Supérieure d'Electricité and made a successful career in his chosen field.

What happened in Grenoble was typical of what was happening all over France which was now completely in the hands of the Germans. The French police, which had been independent until then, at least in the non-occupied zone, were now entirely controlled by the S.S. or the "French Milice". The French milice, founded on January 30, 1943 by Laval, was a collaborationist political and paramilitary force, made up of volunteers who were more akin to gangsters than to officers of law and order. Its members had been recruited among petty thieves, murderers, and pimps. The milice was headed by Joseph Darnand, a French Nazi.

Armed by the Germans, it was doing beautiful work for the Gestapo, arresting Jews and putting them in concentration camps, arresting members of the Resistance and shooting them. Under Darnand's authority the resisters were tried immediately by a three judge panel. These panels were not made up of professional judges, but officers of the regular police or leaders of the milice who acted anonymously. There was no defense counsel, no written transcript of the verdict which could not be appealed and the sentence, invariably death, was carried out immediately. The milice was responsible for kidnappings and premedited murders. Among its most well known victims, murdered in cold blood, were Georges Mandel and Jean Zay, both former ministers under the French Republic, and Victor Basch and his wife, respectively 80 and 79 years old. For years Basch had been the President of the League for the Rights of Man, an organization dedicated to protect the principles of the Revolution of 1789, and a pillar of support for civil rights. Uncle Fernand was its secretary for many years.

Darnand underestimated the force of the Resistance, for he thought that the resisters were a small minority of the French population, represented mostly by the communists, the freemasons and the Jews. In fact, by the end of 1943, because of the worsening political and economic conditions, a large segment of the French people, who had not previously taken an active part in resisting the Germans turned toward helping the underground forces that had become assiduous in its efforts to thwart Nazi control. A brutal civil war had now broken out between the milicians and the resisters. Everyday, bodies were found on the streets with a slip of paper. Depending on who had been murdered, it read either "Death to collaborators", or Death to a Jew lover." In all France, ambushes, murders, reprisals, volleys of firing squads, kidnappings and deportations were the order of the day.

It was the time when good guys were in jail and the bad guys on the street, when men and women were denounced to the Germans by people they believed to be their friends, and when families were torn apart in disputes over their allegiances. The mass of people, leading a life of gray despair and constant fear, finally abandoned the codes of behavior of an organized society that no longer existed.

In preparation for the forecasted landing of the Allied forces the underground turned its activities against the Germans, though it was very conscious that the price for killing German soldiers was extremely high. For each German soldier killed one hundred hostages were shot. Sometimes whole villages in which Germans had been killed were razed and their populations massacred. It has been estimated that by the end of war, close to thirty thousand hostages were shot. In spite of its best intentions to save French lives, it became necessary for the Resistance to sabotage the military operations of the Germans. Among these activities were the blowing up of trains, factories and prisons. This could be easily understood. But movie houses were also dynamited. Why? I have no idea. But it happened in Lyon, the second city of France and at the time the headquarters of most of the French resistance networks. While I did not actually see one of the biggest movie houses in this town blow up, I came close, and could even been killed. Two hours before the explosion, attempting to kill time between two trains, I was inside that building watching one of the famous movies of Jean Renoir, The Imprint of One God. Was the underground trying to get rid of Klauss Barbie, the Butcher of Lyon, who could have been there? If it was, it missed. But I remember seeing a lot of S.S.officers in the movie house that day.

That same night I heard a series of explosions. The underground was carrying out its sabotage of trains carrying military equipment and ammunition. These trains, driven by Frenchmen, were selected to be blown up at special locations. Dynamite sticks were laid under the tracks a few minutes before the trains were to pass. After quite a few trains had been destroyed, the Germans thought of a way to prevent this. They ordered that each train must be preceded by a locomotive to run one minute before the train. If there were dynamite sticks under the track, the first engine would be blown up, but not the train. But this did not occur. The first locomotive passed unharmed; the train still blew up. The underground with the complicity of French Railworkers somehow devised a successful plan for blowing up the second locomotive but not the first, which remained a mystery to the Germans throughout the war. The first engine passing over the dynamite that had been laid on the tracks detonated it by delayed action. What the exact mechanism was I do not know. The engineer and the fireman of the train engine knew in advance where the dynamite had been laid. They jumped from the engine far enough in advance so that the train passed by them before exploding. The engineer and the fireman were officially declared dead and a mock funeral was performed a few days later. In fact, both of them surfaced under false names in some other part of France ready to do the same thing once more. Sometimes one of them was hurt after jumping from the train and was picked up by the underground and hidden for several months. Blowing up trains became a very skillful art, and played a very important role in preventing quite a few German troops from reaching the Normandy Coast in the first weeks of the allied invasion. Eisenhower recognized this in one of his speeches and in his memoirs. Yet, as some historian remarked later, as successful as the sabotage of French trains was, no attempt was ever made to stop convoys of deportees from Drancy, the famous French transit camp for Jews and political prisoners on the road to gas chambers. Since the administration of Drancy had been taken over by the Gestapo, the convoys were rolling more and more often. Whatever the objective of the sabotage was or could have been, the price that the French railworkers paid was high. Many of them were arrested, tortured, and sometimes killed by the Germans who became wise to the fact that the railworkers themselves were part of the underground.

In early 1944, a few months before D-Day, the French people were living in political and social turmoil. The war was not going well for the Germans. Soviet troops were slowly moving westward, and in trying to contain their advance the German army was losing a lot of men. Things were not any better on the Italian battlefront, since the Allies were at the door of Rome and it was just a matter of time until they would invade Northern Europe. Even though it was clear that the Third Reich would eventually lose the war, it had not given up the battle. Life for people of Europe under the "Nazi boot" became very harsh. They were hungry, cold and sick after suffering a terrible winter. All the agricultural and economic resources of France, Belgium, Holland, and Denmark, had been taken by the Germans to support their war effort. Little was left for these countries but the hope that the Allies would soon land. To top it all, every day the Anglo-Americans were bombing French cities killing French people who would never see the liberation of their country.

Things were very bad, but for Gilles and me, the thing that made us decide to escape from France was the real possibility of being sent to Germany as slave laborers. This was the straw that broke the camel's back. Since February of 1943 compulsory labor laws, known as STO, short for Service du Travail Obligatoire, had forced French people to be drafted to help the German war effort. Deep in Germany, the cities were bombed daily. In order to keep his factories running and still have enough soldiers for battle, Hitler found it necessary to replace German factory workers with workers from occupied Europe. It has been estimated that throughout the war four millions of them were sent to Germany where they were treated as slaves. According to statistics, a million French men and women were sent to Germany during the war, and forty thousands of them died there. By August 1943, Pierre Laval who masterminded the STO, was no longer eager to send so many French people to work for the Germans. As a result he slowed down the French police in their efforts to" recruit STO volunteers." The S.S., who by now dictated everything, including who was to be a member of the French Government, resorted to kidnapping in order to get the workers the Reich needed. They blocked streets in towns and cities and went from house to house picking up men and women 18 to 25 years old. Therefore, like every other young French man or woman, Gilles and I were now living in fear of being kidnapped by the S.S. and sent to Germany to work there.

There were only two ways by which young people could escape slave labor in the German war factories, one of which was to join the French Forces of the Interior (F.F.I.). These were guerillas whose camps were in forested mountains or plateaus high in the center of France, in the Alps or Pyrenees. The mountains made it harder, but not impossible, for the Germans to fight them with heavy artillery and tanks. The F.F.I. were supplied with guns and ammunition by the Allies. Unfortunately the airdrops were not always sufficient and many F.F.I. died waiting for supplies which never came or came too late. This was the fate of the maquis of the Vercors in Savoy.

A second way to escape labor in German factories was to flee from France through either Spain or Switzerland. The preferred route was across the Spanish border, because once in Spain it was possible to go directly to North Africa, England or the United States. But crossing the Spanish border was very dangerous, not only because of the possibility of being caught and shot by the German guards, but also because, Spain, being an ally of Germany, might choose to send any escapee back to France putting him or her in the hands of the Gestapo. In spite of these dangers, many men and women escaped from France through Spain: members of the Allied Airforces who had the unhappy experience of being shot down in continental Europe; members of the underground, of intelligence groups, and political figures.

Escapees, helped by the local underground, were either hidden in car trunks or railway baggage cars or they scaled the Pyrenees through passes ranging from 4200 to 9000 feet high. Some never made it. They were caught by German border guards or died under their bullets. Others died of fatigue, injuries from falls in the mountains or the cold, particularly from frost bitten toes which became gangrenous. Yet, because of the worsening social and economical conditions in France, the flight through Spain intensified in the early months of 1944. Many young men, a few young women and some older men, took the chance of dying crossing the border. Among them were Gilles and I. It was March 1944. We were now alone. Our parents and our friends had gone their separate ways. It was time to go.

PART 7
THE ESCAPE

Chapter 20

From The Alps To The Pyrenees

My native land, good night.

Lord Byron

Our 1944 escape was planned by our parents. They had moved in January from Le Monêtier to Saillans, near Valence in the Rhone Valley. They did this because too many people in the village of Le Monêtier knew who they were and they risked being betrayed by someone. When our parents reached Saillans, they changed their identities and became Mr.and Mrs. Gout.

Early in March, they decided that it was time for Gilles and me to leave the country. Through excellent friends they had contacted Emile d'Astier, chief of one of the most important network of the Resistance and later a member of de Gaulle's cabinet. His staff arranged help for us to cross the Spanish border. So, one afternoon in early March 1944, word was passed to us to leave Briançon by train and join our parents at Saillans.

The next morning we took a few things in knapsacks and rode our bicycles to the railway station. We left without saying anything to anyone. Our friend, Gilbert Gout reproached this later, for he would have loved to come with us.

Our journey had started. Because of its special location close to the Italian border, the railway station was always closely watched by the Gestapo. The day we left was no exception. There had been a lot of guerilla activity in the mountains that week and the Gestapo was more eager than ever to find its enemies. As we were passing the control point, we saw a man we knew being arrested. It was Julien B., a famous French writer, who had stayed in the same hotel in Le Monêtier as my parents did. His lady friend, who was with him, was disheveled, in tears and seeing us ran towards us shouting: "They arrested Julien". Gilles, not wanting to draw attention to us, answered: "Lady, we do not know you." And we hurried to board the train after having put our bicycles in the baggage car at the end of the train. Thinking about the arrest of this man, we entered a compartment with heavy hearts. Years later I learned that Julien B., fortunately, had been released from an Austrian detention camp two weeks after his arrest.

We did not have any problem during the trip from Briancon to Saillans. The landscape was beautiful as usual, but we did not have any inclination to admire it. We were too nervous, wondering what would happen in the next few days. On the platform at Saillans we saw Father waiting for us. I thought he had changed his physical appearance. I was right, for he had shaved his mustache that he had for forty years. The three of us rode our bicycles to a little house where Mother was waiting. Some lunch was ready and we ate it with great pleasure. Then the four of us rode our bicycles out into the country where we were given instructions on how to reach the Pyrenees. These instructions were given to us in an open field so that no one could hear our conversation.

We were told by our parents that we were to go to Marseilles, where we would meet a lady who would bring us to Perpignan, a big French city and harbor at the foothills of the Pyrenees. There we would pass a few

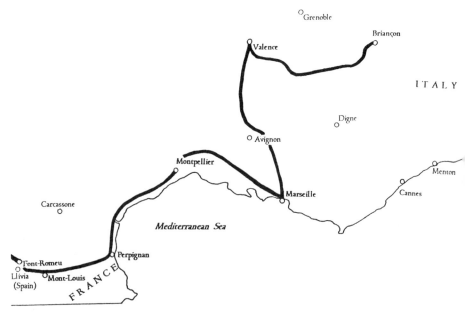

Our Trip from Briançon to Font Romeu by train

days being prepared for our trip over the Pyrenees. Our parents were nervous but not emotional. Obviously they did not want us to feel bad about leaving them. However, it was obvious that we would not be back home for quite a while and that they did not have any idea about our future and theirs. The only advice our parents could give us had to be very general and brief, and can be summarized in one sentence:" Be careful of women and do not join the Airforce. Both are very dangerous." Then, Father gave us some money, always a good thing to have.

As we were coming back to our parents' temporary home, a gust of wind threw a small tree branch right into the spokes of the front wheel of my bicycle, and I flew over the handle bars. I landed on my head. My brow just above my right eye was bleeding. My parents, now really worried, led me to a physician in town. Though I walked on my own power, I was unconscious for thirty minutes. I did not remember what happened from the time of the fall to the time I reached the physician's office. The physician examined me, but did not want to suture me. He was afraid that if I bore a bandage the Germans would believe that I had been hit by a bullet and would undoubtedly arrest me, believing I was an F.F.I., who had been wounded during a battle with them. The bleeding stopped by itself and in a few days I healed, but I still wear a distinctive scar above my right eye.

The next morning Gilles and I bid good bye to our parents. It was rather a strange farewell for Father and Mother rarely expressed their emotions and, though they were not sure they would ever see us again, there were no tears in their eyes or ours. The four of us knew that the wisest thing for Gilles and I was to leave France and escape this hellish place that was once the land of freedom. I always suspected that Mother cried after our departure. After all her two boys, her only children, were now gone and she had no idea when we would be back.

Without our bicycles this time, we took a slow train to Valence, an important city in the Rhone valley, and then a faster train to Marseilles. In its main railway station we met a young lady about 30 years old, who was waiting for us below the "Great Clock". She recognized us from a photo given by my mother to the underground. Soon the three of us were on a train to Perpignan, a hundred miles from Marseilles. She had with her a suitcase which we learned later, contained not only some of her clothes, but also military information to be given to the Allies. Suitcases were often opened by the French police who were checking for black market goods. The best way not to have your suitcase opened by the police was to put it on the racks above the head of German officers, since the police would believe the suitcase belonged to one of them. That is what she did. As a matter of fact, because our new friend was very pretty, one of the German army officers helped her to put the suitcase on the rack. Then, she left the compartment and joined us in the hallway. Gilles and I were astonished at her coolness. After all if the suitcase had been opened and its ownership determined, she would have been arrested, tortured, and probably killed. Smiling she talked to us about the weather and the beautiful sunset in the western horizon. Our guide was sharing with us the fact that the beauty of nature can be enjoyed in the midst of a great deal of human suffering. She was a very energetic and smart woman, a real leader, who, after the liberation of France, was elected a council member of the town of Cannes which since the war has become so famous for being the center of an international film festival.

A few miles from the important French city of Perpignan the train slowed down crossing the old rusted bridge over the Tet river. We were now in the lovely French province of Roussillon, with its highly fertile plains, bordered to the South by the Pyrenees which are dominated there by the snow capped summit of Mt. Canigou. A few minutes later we got off the train and walked into the railway station of Perpigan which Salvador Dali jokingly said was the center of the world.

In the railway station there was a tremendous amount of activity which was carefully watched over by the police. Because of the town's location, so close to Spain, the German police kept a close eye on everyone, and with good reason, for thousands of people, French and non-French, had used Perpignan as a transit point on their escape route to Spain. To go out of the railway station we had to pass a police check point manned by French Gendarmes. No problem! We presented our I.D.Cards bearing our real names and soon, accompanied by our guide, we were walking down Avenue Maréchal Petain to the Place de Catalogne, passing in front of the Gestapo headquarters. Before the war Avenue Maréchal Petain was called Avenue de la Gare; now, it is called Avenue General de Gaulle. After the liberation, every street, avenue and square bearing the name of Pétain was renamed Avenue de Gaulle, reflecting political changes.

The three of us went two blocks north and walked up to a third floor apartment. There we met two ladies in their twenties. It was supper time and we got something to eat. Gilles and I were told that we would be in the apartment for three days, the time needed to make false I.D. cards. As a precaution we did not go out during those three days. We did not get bored, for we soon found out that the two younger women were involved in the making of cigarettes that they smuggled across the Spanish border. They welcomed our help in rolling tobacco strips and wrapping them in a very thin cigarette paper. At the end of the three days my brother and I had become experts. We learned that the people in Perpignan, as well as in the Roussillon, never tell you that they are French, but rather Catalan, a name which is more than an echo of the Spanish Province of Catalonia, which nestles along the same coast but on the Southern slope of the Pyrenees. Saddled across the mountains, Catalonia was once united and independent, with its own language, literature, and traditions. But since 1659, the Catalans of the Roussillon have been French. In that year the province was annexed to France as the result of the treaty of the Pyrenees. This treaty marked the victory of France in a 30 year war with Spain. We learned from our guides that the old city of Perpignan had a long and complicated history, including paying allegiance to the Kings of Aragon, Majorca and finally of France. Its historical past, we were told, explains why the town has a distinctly Spanish air about it.

During our stay in the apartment, the lady in charge of our escape, the one we met in Marseilles, let us call her Mrs.C., gave us instructions for our trip: what to expect and what to say if we were caught by the Germans. The best advice we got was to keep our mouth shut until we were out of Spain, for it was well known that in Spain Gestapo agents were plentiful, always on the lookout for information about their enemies, who they were and their whereabouts. The Gestapo was not bashful about kidnapping or killing political figures, agents for the Allies and members of the underground. We found later how wise she had been to warn us.

The third day, early in the morning, we were given our new I.D.cards. They looked perfectly authentic. They had our pictures which had been taken the day before, our fingerprints and the official stamps. Our name, though, had been changed to Cordes and our residence was given as Font Romeu, a well known French ski resort, seven miles north of the Spanish border. The reason for such a home address was that no one could official-ly reach the Spanish border unless he or she either had official business or lived there. Since the end of 1943 German troops had replaced the French border guards who were helping people to escape. To insure that fewer people escaped through the mountains, the German authorities had declared the counties near the border a forbidden zone. We were soon to find out that the border was well patrolled and checkpoints were numerous.

We were now psychologically and physically ready to go. We were not told what our road of escape was to be though we had an idea that it would be across the frontier valley of La Cerdagne. We ate a small breakfast. Mrs.C. gave us her last instructions. She bade us good luck and kissed us good bye. One of the young ladies, the one with dark hair and black eyes, was to guide us across the border, but we were told that it was imperative that we were to ignore her during our train trip to Font Romeu. We would not talk to her as a precaution if any of us was caught by the Germans before reaching Font Romeu. If Gilles and I were caught, the young lady would be free to return to Perpignan. If she were caught, we would be free to attempt crossing the Spanish border another time.

Chapter 21

The Little Yellow Train
Crossing The Spanish Border

The courage mounteth with occasion.

SHAKESPEARE

In the early morning we walked back to the railway station of Perpignan to take the train to the very picturesque town of Villefranche de Confluent at the base of the Massif Canigou, a series of high Pyrenean peaks over-looking both France to the north and Spain to the South. We checked the schedule under the large clock and then went through the tunnel under the first set of railway tracks in order to reappear on the platform on the other side of the tracks. The train was already there. Would we be able to get into it? There were so many people. Gilles and our guide managed to squeeze through the door and into the hallway. I succeeded in being the last pas-senger in the car and the door was literally slammed behind my back. I was pressed against a man about 40 years old who moved slightly to give me more room. We smiled to each other and started a conversation about the niceties of overcrowded trains and the beautiful weather we had so far this year. This type of conversation was not too compromising.

The trip to Villefranche de Confluent took about fifty minutes. The train out of Perpignan followed the meanderings of the Tet river, stopping at the small towns of Le Soler, Millas, Isle sur Tet, Vinca, Prades, and Ria. It passed through rich alluvial farmland that yields fine fruit and vegeta-bles, which, because of their freshness and of their early appearance in the Spring, won ready sale in the Paris markets. The peach trees were already in bloom, casting a pinkish glow in the landscape. As we approached closer to the mountains, we could admire vineyards on the ruddy slopes of the hills. Tended as carefully as flower-gardens, the grapevines were already budding, promising succulent grapes in the fall.

We arrived at the station of Villefranche, located outside the town, on the bank of the Tet river. That particular day we had no time to visit this walled-in medieval town with its narrow and tortuous streets. This was too bad, for it had kept all its charm as my wife and I found out forty years later. Villefranche was originally built by the Count of Cerdagne in the 11th century, and fortifed by the uquibitous Vauban. Its fortications are still standing, with their gateways and bastions. The massive 12th century church is flanked by old houses which bask in the placid atmosphere of a place once strategically important, but now neglected and sleepy.

To reach Font Romeu in the middle of the province of Cerdagne we had to change at Villefranche and take a very special train, called the little yellow train. It still exists as it was in 1911 when it was first put in operation. It is a very special train because it rides on a narrow track one meter wide instead of the regular one of one meter and forty four centimeters on which the other French trains run. It is also special because there is a third rail, an electrified one, that permits the little yellow train to climb very steep slopes to reach the Cerdagne plateau, a very beautiful, but very isolated region. The electric power which lifts the little yellow train comes from the mighty waters of the upper gorges of the valley as if the mountains were sending out a helping welcoming hand. The plateau can also be reached by a road with many switchbacks, but during the German occupation the road was not used much by the French, for, as I mentioned before, they did not have any cars to drive then. The only way to reach the Cerdagne was really to take the little yellow train.

This train climbs from Villefranche to Mount-Louis at a height of approximately 3300 feet traveling less than 18 miles on the slopes of the Valley of La Tet either on the right or the left of the river. After Mount Louis the little yellow train reaches the highest point of its trip, the pass of La Perche at an altitude of 5,000 feet. Going westward it reaches Font Romeu and from then on the little yellow train lazily meanders across the province of Cerdagne, circumventing the Spanish enclave of Llivia, going down slowly to La Tour de Carol, its western French terminal station.

When we took the little yellow train on that particular day in March of 1944 at the Villefranche station, there were only a few passengers and we were able to find seats. To better understand what follows, I have to add that the railway cars of the little yellow train—and this is still true today—did not have compartments as did the regular French railway cars. There was only one partition in the middle of the car with a door that leads from one part of the car to the next. On each side of the middle aisle, there were six blocks of seats. Each block had four seats, each two facing the other two.

Gilles and I chose to sit near a window, facing each other, because we wanted to admire the strikingly beautiful landscape. Our guide was close by. The little yellow train soon started and immediately we became aware of its rusticity. The ride was far from comfortable, for the train did not roll smoothly on the rails. It gnashed and shook, though it was going only twenty miles an hour. At every turn we had to cling to something.

Well, that particular day, train comfort was the least of our worries. We had not left Villefranche for more than three minutes when we heard the fateful sentence, "Papers, please. "I turned around and I could not believe my eyes. The man who was asking to check every one's papers was the very man with whom I just talked for quite a while on the other train. He was a non-uniformed gestapo agent. I became instantly very nervous. Soon he came to our seats and smiled. I offered to show him our papers, but he declined to see them. He said: "Good morning again. Is this your brother?" As I nodded, he added:"Great, I'll see you." After he left, checking other people's papers, Gilles gave me an inquiring look and softly said: "I did not know you had friends in the Gestapo." Luck was obviously on our side.

Three minutes later, my "new Gestapo friend" left our railway car for the next one. As he was doing so, he turned around and waved good-bye to me. By that time another German agent, this time in uniform, had entered our railway car. When he came to our seats, he asked me if I was a friend of the other agent (he had obviously seen us waving good-bye). I told him I was. Again we did not have to show our papers.

Gilles and I relaxed for a while admiring the landscape, the narrowing of the valley into a gorge which seemed to end so abruptly that it looked as if there was no way ahead except perpendicularly up the peak. But the gorge continued curving around the mountain and soon we reached the railway station of Sardinya. We found it to be another security checkpoint. This time I had no "friends" in the German police. A man in a black uniform was soon checking our I.D.cards. For some reason he did not think they were authentic. He checked to see if the ink was fresh by exposing the cards to a beam of light. His check took a few seconds, but these seconds were the longest seconds of our lives. We were not sure at all that we were going to pass that test. This time, it would be Gilles' turn to save us. He said to me in a voice loud enough to be heard by the German agent :" Look at the grapevines. The buds surely grew quite a bit in the last two weeks." The trick worked. The German policeman looked at us again and decided we were indeed from that part of the country and gave us back our papers. We were lucky. The grapevines had indeed grown fast that year and, though there were few in the gorge, some happened to be close to our rail-way car window and Gilles was able to make his wise remark. Our physical appearance must have also played some role in the decision of the German agent, for Gilles and I had dark hair, with a complexion that reminds one of the Mediterranean people. We could easily pass for inhabitants of the Pyrenees. Yet, it would have been so easy for the SS agent to find that we were not. We did not speak Spanish, nor the dialect of the region. Indeed, we were very lucky for this was the last checkpoint and we never had to show our forged papers again.

The train started again climbing slowly. We passed the village of Joncet which used to be very important because that was where all the

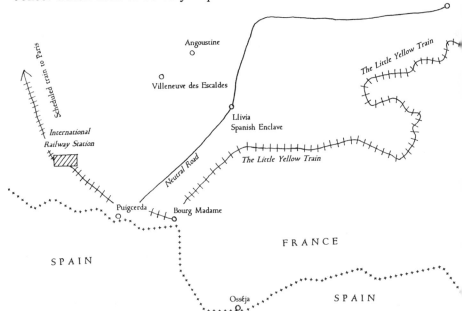

Escape by foot and oxcart from Font Romeu to Puigcerda
From Font Romeu to Llivia (walking)
From Llivia to Puigcerda (ox cart)

iron and manganese ores extracted from the surrounding mountains were loaded on railway cars. Above that village, the valley starts to narrow considerably. The little yellow train leaves the river bed to climb on the South side of the valley. The slope is steep. After about six miles we arrived at Olette, the township seat, perched above the railway tracks. Now, the valley narrows even more. Soon after the village of Nyers the two sides of the valley practically come together, being only as wide as the river. We went through numerous tunnels. Though the valley soon after becomes a little wider, we went through more tunnels and over viaducts striking in their originality and their beauty. Again we crossed the river and arrived at the station which is practically on the top of Fontpederouse, a village that seems to fall from the railway station down to the river below. More tunnels. We arrived at Santo where we crossed the river again this time on a splendid suspension bridge, 250 feet above the river. The train was still climbing, this time through a beautiful pine forest. Crossing another viaduct we abandoned the valley and arrived on a plateau at the base of the fortified town of Mount Louis, which played an important historical role in keeping the region in the hands of France.

Mount Saint Louis, formerly the capital of the French Cerdagne, brags of being the highest European town served by a railway (5,135 feet) and of being the coldest French town. Its ramparts stand as solidly as when they were built, but now one finds vegetable gardens and tennis courts in its moat. The town is still a military garrison proud of its past. Statues of two military heroes adorn the square. One is of General Dagobert, who led the Revolutionary armies successfully against the Spaniards in 1793, but died of wounds at Mount Saint Louis. The other is of Marshal Joffre, Commander in chief during World War I, who as a major in 1892 and 1893 was in command of the Saint Louis garrison.

Soon after leaving Mount Louis, the train climbs up through brown meadows toward the pass of La Perche. It goes from the North Side to the South side of the pass, then reaches the Cerdagne plateau. I found this landscape striking. Cerdagne looks like a valley with its rim of mountains, whose crests are all nearly on a level with the Canigou. Yet, the floor of the Cerdagne is itself so high that the surrounding crests give only a fraction of the sense of height that isolates Canigou from the plain of the Roussillon. I was also struck by the fact that the rivers had changed direction. Instead of running down toward the Mediterranean sea, they were now flowing toward Spain, disappearing obviously through a mountain pass I could not see. I then understood why this land was the favorite escape route across Spain. The other passes across the Pyrenees are far higher, more difficult to reach, and weatherwise more treacherous.

The train was now climbing westward on the flank of the glacial plateau until it reached Bolquere, the highest railway station in France at about 5,500 feet. A few minutes later we were at the station of Font Romeu-Odello at the base of the hill that the town of Font Romeu overlooks. We could not see it from the station, which was just as well since we did not have time to visit it. We left the train without any problem, for no policeman checked our papers. We waited a few minutes and when no one was around, we rejoined our guide who was standing a few feet from the station. By that time, we had become very anxious to cross the Spanish border, still not sure of what would become of us once we did it.

Our guide led us across numerous brown grassy and rocky fields. The vegetation was brown because it was far too cold and too early in the year for anything to be growing. The ground could have been covered with snow in those early March days, but fortunately for us there was none. We walked without any trouble for seven miles until we found ourselves on a dirt road, a short distance from the French town of Augustine. Before reaching the town, we were to leave the road walking to the left across a plateau, called Las Puntas. The northern edge of the plateau was the border between France and the Spanish enclave of Llivia. The town of Llivia itself nestled at the bottom of the southern slope of the plateau. Llivia, we soon found out, was our objective. If we could reach it, we would be in Spain, having taken our first step towards freedom.

How this town became an enclave is interesting, for it is the ironic result of hair splitting by treaty makers. According to the 1659 Treaty of the Pyrenees that restored peace between Spain and France, the villages, but not the towns of the Upper Cerdagne, were ceded to France. But Llivia, the ancient capital of the region, held a charter of a town, and though it was a mile within French territory and included barely four square miles of territory, Spain would not give it up, and did not, and Spanish it remained. It is connected with Spain by a shoestring of a neutral road over French soil. Being an enclave, surrounded by French villages, the town became, and still is, a haunt for smugglers. It has also been historically a favorite escape route for political refugees. For instance, during the Spanish Civil War, many Spaniards took that route northward to escape Franco. During World War II, those who were fleeing Nazi Europe took that route southward to reach Spain. In 1944, the border around Llivia was heavily controlled by the German guards and Gilles and I were taking quite a chance.

We were still on the dirt road leading to Augustine when an old Frenchman, 300 feet away, who was cleaning the road with a large broom called to us: "Hey, you boys, if you want to go to Augustine, it is easier to take this short cut. "We told him we were not going to Augustine. He guessed right away that we were attempting to cross the border and he shouted: "Be careful. Today, the Germans are with dogs. I usually see them from here. If you see my broom going back and forth, that means go for it. If you see that I have stopped moving my broom,it means there is too much danger, go back on the road. Try another time."

His broom was going back and fourth and the three of us run over the plateau. Half way our guide, indicating a western direction, told us: "This is the way."I had a gut feeling that she was wrong, because she was pointing to rocky grounds devoid of trees (see picture). It was hard for me to believe that a village could be located in a place where there was no evidence of running water. I told her she was lost. Looking around I decided on the spur of the moment that we should go South. There were a few trees on the edge of the plateau, an indication that there might be some water around. There was no time to argue with our guide. Gilles, who generally never believed that I could be right in anything, this time did believe me, and followed me leaving the young woman behind. Running at full speed, we were soon at the edge of the plateau overlooking a small village in the valley. A few hundred yards below the edge clinging to the hill, were a few houses. When we reached the first house, we asked the woman in it if we were in Llivia. She answered that we were. We felt so relieved. In fact, intuitively, we had gone the exact favorite path that smugglers had used for centuries. Forty years later, in the town of Mount Louis, I met a Frenchman in his late sixties, who told me that during the German occupation he had smuggled, among other things, car tires from France to Spain by letting them roll down that very hill.

The young lady, our guide, had followed us and a few minutes later the three of us went down the hill and reached the center of the town, where we found a small cafe. Drinking hot coffee, we said good bye to our guide who was returning to France. Neither that day nor the next did Gilles or I wonder much about why she seemed not to know the location of Llivia when we were walking on the Las Puntas plateau. We were in Llivia and at that time we did not care. We simply assumed that she became lost.

Yet, this assumption was not a valid one. Here was a woman who made her living by smuggling and guiding people across the Spanish border who got lost in broad daylight. This did not make any sense. The answer came to me years later when Gilles, Mother, and I were sitting in the living room of her home in Berkeley, California. That day we were reminiscing about our escape and I suddenly rejected the idea that our guide had been lost. I was suddenly sure that she was a double agent. She had been paid directly by the underground and indirectly by our parents, to guide us through the border. She could also have been paid by the Germans to deliver us into their hands. My suspicion was never confirmed because we never saw her again. However, when I came back on the Plateau of Las Puntas the second time, in 1986, I found the very spot where she had pointed out to us the "false" direction to Llivia. Following it, I found myself on the road to Augustine, a few feet from a shepherd cabin, the very place where we were told by the old man with his broom that the German guards and their dogs had been stationed forty years before. Hence, I believe now that our young guide had indeed been a double agent and I wonder how many people she handed back to the Germans that way. So, once more, we had been very lucky. Lucky, to have had a knowledge of the topography of mountains gained through our experience in the Alps, to know where villages are located, and to have an excellent inborn sense of direction. We safely crossed the border because it seems that I have a magnet in the brain like pigeons do and because I do not to have a blind trust in mountain guides.

It did not take us long to see the whole town of Llivia which has only 800 inhabitants. But it is an interesting town with its well known balconied streets, its fortified church, and its pharmacy, believed to be one of the oldest in Spain. Llivia, being an enclave in France, we had to reach Spain proper. To do this, we had to take the neutral road that led to the Spanish town of Puigcerda, a distance of two miles. The word " neutral" meant that people could go on that road without being checked by the German or the Spanish police. However, not willing to take any risk we asked the owner of the only hotel in Llivia if he had any advice to give us.

He advised us to find a farmer willing to transport us in a hay cart. Hidden in the hay, hopefully we would not be seen by anyone. We took his advice, hoping that no one in Llivia would betray us. Before continuing our trip we decided to rest for a few hours and to do a few things that needed to be done, namely, hiding our money in our clothes, keeping out a few pesetas for the next few days. To my astonishment Gilles became an expert with needles and thread. We also decided to take back our own identities, gambling that we had definitely escaped the German police. Then, after having eaten a decent lunch, -I cannot remember what we ate, but the food was good-we went looking for someone to take us along the neutral road. We found one man right away who was eager to get a few pesetas for his trouble. We and our few belongings were put under some hay in an ox cart and we were on our way. But a few minutes later the cart stopped and we heard our driver talking in Spanish to a man whom we could not see. Was he a German soldier? Would our driver betray us for a few pesetas? All kinds of thoughts were passing through our mind. We could feel in our necks our blood being pumped at maximum pressure and we could hear strange noises in our guts. Well, the cart suddenly was on its way and thirty minutes later we were in the Spanish town of Puigcerda. We had made it.

CHAPTER 22

Guests In Spain

A closed mouth catches no flies.

CERVANTES

We had no time and no desire to visit the Spanish town of Puigcerda which was founded by the King of Aragon, Alphonso II, as the capital of Cerdagne in 1177. This very old town stands on a hill in the center of a mountain-girt plain and now has a population of about 6,000. Not speaking Spanish, we decided to surrender to the Spanish police who interrogated us in French for an hour. It became apparent that the policemen were far more interested in how much money we had than in our political convictions. As a matter of fact, they confiscated our pesetas, at least most of them. Soon after, they put us in a special jail. It was a villa outside Puigcerda which belonged to a rich man, but had been taken over by the Spanish government to house escapees. It was a transit jail, where people stayed for a while.

Reading the inscriptions on the walls we concluded that the villa had housed many English and American aviators. Some of these inscriptions were not encouraging, because they were telling us how long these aviators had been there, sometimes for months. The police had told us we were in jail for only the week end. We started doubting their word. The other escapees did not believe that we would stay there only two days. What they did not know and what we did not know was that young people who were less than 21 years old were not staying in jail any more. This was an economic, not a humane, arrangement, made between the Spanish government and the Allies, which dated to only a few months before.

The reader might wonder why and how Spain could be allied to Germany, but relatively friendly to the escapees from Nazis. Well, Franco did not do this from the kindness of his heart. He was doing this because his people were starving. For every able body that he was releasing from jails, he was getting 200 pounds of wheat from the United States. Gilles and I must have been exchanged for two bags of wheat.

During the week-end we slept on cots, were fed and read some books we had taken with us. Well, Monday morning came and at eight-o clock, believe it or not, a Spanish policeman told us he was going to escort us to Figueras by train. This policeman, who spoke some French, was a young friendly fellow. We asked him some questions about what was to be our destiny in Spain. But he did not seem to know. We left our week-end jail, walked over to the railway station. We had been lucky again, this time to be teenagers and not being in jail for a long time. We were on our way to Figueras a few miles south of the French border. This old town, dominated by the fort of Castillo de St.Fernando, is the birthplace of Salvador Dali.

Though we were accompanied by a policeman we were free to walk and talk on the train. We behaved like regular passengers, and we soon discovered that some young women on the train were interested in us. It was a nice feeling and a new experience for us, for during our teen age life, passed under the Italian and German occupation, we had little occasion to meet young women,as there were no social gatherings of any kind and night curfews were strictly enforced.

These Spanish women were curious about us and asked a lot of questions, but since we did not speak Spanish our policeman had to do the interpreting. Being young himself and finding the girls pretty, he did not seem to mind the task. He made a few mistakes in translating. One of them brought laughter from the young women. He had been asked how much younger than me my brother was. Instead of saying fifteen months,

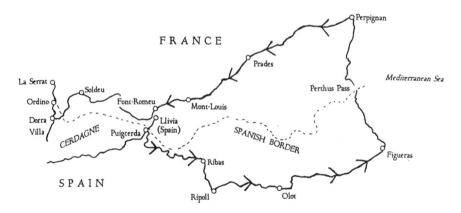

Perpignan to Figueras (Overview)

he said five. Obviously, he knew little about the human gestation period.

We soon discovered how poor the Spanish people were. Our police-man did not have any money for lunch. We left the train at Ripoll and we invited him to share a light meal with us. The three of us ate a nice omelet with mushrooms and drunk some wine. At that point we had a new friend. We took the train again and the rest of the trip was nice. We reached the city of Figueras late in the afternoon and were delivered to the authorities in charge of the city jail.

The next few days were rather bleak: we were back in jail. This time a real jail. The cells were small with cement walls, iron bars and steel doors. The beds were broken and filthy and so were the floors. The jail was very crowded. There were a tremendous number of escapees from all over Europe, Holland, Belgium, France, and even Poland. There were American and English airforce men. There were even a few Russian and German deserters. English was the common language in that jail. Those who did not know English could always find someone who could trans-late what they were saying into English. Sometimes the translation had to be done through two or even three persons. But we managed to commu-nicate one way or the other.

We shared our small cell with two Frenchmen, one about 35 years old, the other about 52 years old. We soon discovered that they were part of the underground. The younger was a member of the British Intelligence. The other was the head of a regional underground in the Alps. Both had to leave France in a hurry because the Germans had discovered their true identities. In technical terms, they were "burnt". They had crossed the Pyrenees and now they were in jail with us. They told us interesting sto-ries which had to do with their underground experiences.

The most striking one, at least to me, was told by our newly found friend in the Intelligence Service. It took place in the Fall of 1940. Officially, he was a salesman traveling around occupied France. One evening he was eating in Biarritz in a fashionable hotel-restaurant when he noticed that a captain in a Wermacht uniform kept looking at him with-out a smile on his lips. Our friend started to worry. Maybe he had been recognized as a British agent. But the German captain did not move, just sat staring at him. Finally, our friend left his table and went to his bed-room. He was not there three minutes when he heard someone knock at his door. He opened it and there stood the German captain who invited

himself in, closed the door behind him, and sat in a chair, smoking a cigarette. After a few seconds he said in English: " You are working for the
British Intelligence Service, are you not?" Our friend of course denied it.
But it was to no avail. The captain told him: " Your number is 876, but do
not worry for my number is 902. I came for information. "Our friend, of
course, was relieved, but wondered like the rest of us how many British
Agents were German officers, and more important, how many German
citizens were British officers or even part of the Intelligence Service.

Personally, I have known of three cases of German officers who were
British agents. Besides the one just mentioned and the one who was supposed to help me to escape from France in 1942, I knew of another one
in 1940. A young lady who was a friend of Mother had a lover in the
British Army. He disappeared from view during the fall of France. A few
days after the Germans had occupied Paris the young lady was hurriedly
walking along the Champs Elysées when a Wermacht officer with his
monocle caught her eye. He was looking at her with gleaming eyes and
with a loving smile. It was her lover who had metamorphosed himself
into a typical German officer. She left in a hurry wondering on which side
he was fighting the war. A few days later she got a secret note telling her
he was an Allied agent and that he was sure she would keep his secret.
The man was born and raised in Germany and had been drafted into the
German Army. But his parents were English. His heart was with England,
and his mind with the British Intelligence.

The other striking story was told to us by the older Frenchman. One
day, in the Alps, a seventeen year old boy was carrying a suitcase that
contained a large number of maps describing the locations of the German
forces. He had to deliver the suitcase to someone in another town 50 miles
away. To do this, he had to take a train. Entering a compartment, he put
the suitcase, contrary to the instructions he had received, in the net above
the seat he took instead of above the head of someone who knew nothing
of the contents of the suitcase. This was done as a precaution. It prevented the police from discovering the owner of the suitcase and the identity
of an underground agent. The French police, always looking for black
market produces, asked the young man to open the suitcase. He did.
Seeing the maps, the French policeman, called the German police. He
kept the young man inside the compartment by locking the door. The
young man decided to escape through the window just a few minutes

before the train would go through the next tunnel. He was sure he would not be seen because, due to the mandatory black out that affected all Europe, there was complete darkness in the train when it went through a tunnel. The young man knew the railroad journey well and the exact location of every tunnel. Within a small distance of one of these tunnels he pulled down the window and jumped. The train was going at about 25 miles an hour and the only damage that the young man did to himself was to sprain one of his ankles. He was found by a shepherd who fed him for a month. Then, the young man walked back home.

Our French friends thought that, since they were now in Spain, it was safe for them to talk. But this was a mistake as they soon found out. Spain was not free of German agents or sympathizers. Those two Frenchmen, who should have known better, talked too much. Soon the Gestapo learned who they were, and attempted to bring them back to France, hoping that there, under torture, they would release the names of their underground friends. Here is what happened to them when they were in the Figueras jail with us.

We had been locked up in jail for three days when our compatriots were taken out of the cell and led to a special room where two men, speaking French with a British accent, talked to them for an hour. Then, our friends returned to our cell. We asked them what's up. They refused to answer our questions.

Only months after the liberation of France did I learn the subject of the conversation that they had with the two men. The former British Intelligence agent came to Clair Matin, our parents' home in Roquebrune, in the Spring of 1945 and asked to see Gilles and me. Father told him that we were in the United States and asked him why he wanted to see us. He answered that he had befriended us when we were together in jail in Figueras and this friendship saved both his life and the life of another Frenchman. This is the story as told to our father.

The two men who came to see them in the Figueras jail were not British agents, as our friends were led to believe, but Gestapo agents posing as British agents. They told our friends that they would drive them by car to Algeciras- located at the Southern tip of Spain- and from there they could reach Algiers by boat. They were too important people to stay in jail even for a few days. Permission therefore had been granted for their release. They could go immediately. Our friends, however, did not want to go without us. We undoubtedly reminded them of their children and we had developed a strong friendship during those three days. So they insisted that the so- called British agents must take us with them.

Our friends did not suspect for a moment that these two gentlemen were really Gestapo agents and that their true mission was to bring them back to France. So they were somewhat surprised that the "British agents" refused. But, it was not surprising that the Gestapo agents refused to take Gilles and me with them. The car would be too crowded, but more importantly they expected trouble for they knew that young men are not as docile as older men are. They believed that Gilles and I might react violently once we found out that we were on our way back to France. If we attempted to hit the driver as he negotiated a turn around one of those switchbacks, we would have endangered everybody's life, but this would have been of little concern to us since we knew we would have died anyway at the hands of the Gestapo.

And so, because the two Gestapo agents refused to take us in their car, our friends, who wanted so much that Gilles and I should go with them to North Africa, told the two agents they would wait with us in our cell until the Spanish Government would permit all of us to leave. It is only when they reached Algiers three weeks later that they learned that the two agents were not British, but German, and how lucky they had been. Their friendship for two young men had saved their lives.

We stayed four days in the Figueras jail. The fifth day we and many other escapees were put on a train to Barcelona, wondering what the following days would bring.

The trip to Barcelona was not at all pleasant. Gilles and I were handcuffed to each other, so were the other escapees. We talked in French, so the Spanish passengers in the train would know that we were not criminals of some kind, but foreigners in transit in their homeland. The distance between Figueras and Barcelona was not great, about fifty miles, but because our freedom was limited, we found the time going very slowly. The only distraction we had was to observe the landscape which reminded us of the French Riviera.

The train stopped in Gerona, but of course, still handcuffed, we did not leave it. All we could do was to stand in the corridor and look at the town with its numerous churches and its famous cathedral. We finally arrived in Barcelona, where, after being walked two or three blocks, we landed once more in jail. This time, we were put in the basement of the city jail, where we shared a cell with male Spanish law breakers. In the adjoining cells were noisy prostitutes yelling so loudly that we could hear everything they said. This again was a new experience for us. We learned about another side of life that we had not seen yet, and heard Spanish words not generally taught in classes of conversational Spanish.

After being in jail for two hours we were visited by members of the Red Cross who were really representatives of the American Government. They asked us a lot of questions about ourselves. We answered as best we could. A few hours later we were released in the custody of the Red Cross which put us in a room in a private home, and gave us a meal ticket to be used in a small restaurant not too far away. We were to stay under these conditions until we heard from the Red Cross again. We had been given some pocket money, but there was so little of it that we could not buy much with it. Fortunately, our needs were small, and we still had some French money in case of dire need.

We passed fifteen days in Barcelona in rather comfortable surroundings. Our lodging was very adequate. We thoroughly enjoyed the meals we had in the sidewalk restaurant. This is not surprising since after four years of undernourishment, we were not picky eaters. We were very happy not to have our stomachs squeezing any more. The family that lodged us was very nice. The conversation was, of course, limited since we did not speak Spanish and no one in the family spoke French.

Though we were free to roam the streets, we did not attempt to visit Barcelona systematically. I guess we were not in the mood. Now, I regret it since this is a busy metropolis, beautifully situated between the vivid blue Mediterranean sea and purple hills with its striking summit of Tibidado. This harbor city is favored by its climate. The winter temperatures are mild, while the sultry summer heat is tempered by sea breezes. Barcelona is a very old city, dating back from the Carthaginian era. It was once part of the Roman empire, then fell into the hands of the Arabs, and finally was brought into Christendom. Barcelona was for a while the capital of the Catalan -Aragonese monarchy and grew into an important sea port. The charm of this metropolis which lies in its multifaceted heritage, Roman, Arab, Christian, does not seem to have vanished with the industrial modernization that has made Barcelona the richest city in Spain.

During those fifteen days we were in Barcelona Gilles and I walked mostly around the neighborhood where we had our room. Unfortunately, I have little recollection of what we saw. But, there is one thing I still remember vividly. One day, as we walked down a big avenue- I think it was The Paseo de Gracia- we saw young couples, dressed up in beautiful regional clothes, dancing all kinds of Spanish dances in front of a sidewalk restaurant. We thoroughly enjoyed the show, especially the very graceful young ladies who accompanied their dances with castanets. This, of course, is very understandable. We were then young men who, so far, had little opportunity to appreciate the beauty and elegance of the other sex.

A few days later, our older French friends called on us. They were inviting us to see a bullfight. Being on the payroll of the Resistance they had enough money to enjoy life and spare some on their young friends. We accepted. It was our first and last bullfight. We went to the bullring, the one at Plaza de las Arenas. The ring was large. There were a lot of people, dressed in colorful clothes, shouting, gesticulating, having a wonderful time.

Before the corrida started, the audience had to hail Generalissimo Franco. Reluctantly, we got up off our seats and raised our right arm the fascist way and said:" Viva Franco", then we sat down and the spectacle started.

The matador appeared dressed in tight colored pants and a golden shirt. He dedicated the bull that he was going to kill to a beautiful lady, as the audience was throwing all kinds of things in the ring, rice, hats, and even a dead chicken. He raised his arms, smiling, showing his appreciation.

Gilles and I knew nothing about bullfights. The following description is what the Spanish audience was expecting of a true-to-form bullfight. A bullfight consists of four parts: the trial, the sentence, the punishment, and finally the execution. During the trial, the bull is teased by the matador and the peons. They use a cape (a capote) which the bull runs into. The way the bull responds to this teasing teaches the matador the nature of that particular bull, how he moves, favoring either the right or the left, how he uses his horns. In other words what the bull does do when he charges is of utmost importance to the matador who is pulled by two contradictory wishes: he does not want to be gored and at the same time he wants the audience to appreciate his skill and artistry in bull-fighting. If the bull responds favorably to the wish of the matador, he is sentenced to die that afternoon in the arena. That is when the punishment starts. It is the role of the picadors, towering on their padded horses, to weaken the bull by wounding him with long pics. During this act, the music is playing and the crowd is roaring its approval. Then, the banderillos on foot, get as close to the bull as they can, plunge their banderillas into the back of the bull, weakening him as much as possible. Then comes the final act, the execution. The matador now faces the bull alone. This is what everyone is waiting for, he plays with the muletta and the killing of the bull. For some reason that is not too clear, at least to me, the bull charges the muletta and not the man. The matador obviously counts on this, and his skill is to escape just in time from the trajectory of the bull. The man is so sure of himself that after his play with the muletta he walks towards the audience, his back to the bull, which he hopes will not move. This shows how courageous the matador is. Now, it is time for the killing. The matador hides his sword inside the muletta, does a few more tricks with it, and when the beast is at the right time at the right place, the matador executes the bull by thrusting the sword in high up between the shoulders and into the heart. This is the rule. The reason for this rule is that the bull will only lower his head when the matador brings his body within the range of the horns. If done right, the bull staggers a few seconds and then falls dead. The appreciative audience roars its delight and throws more things into the ring. The matador waves to the crowd. During that time the dead bull is pulled on his side by a team of three powerful panached horses that go around the ring at least once, sometimes twice, and finally exit. If the matador has killed the bull elegantly and skillfully, he is rewarded by the gift of the two ears of the beast. He then shows them to the crowd. He bows and is finally carried on the shoulders of his friends. And if this is the last bull to be killed, there will be an overflow of men into the ring, drinking and dancing to the music of the band.

This is what a corrida should be if the bull follows the rules and if the matador is a great one. The bull fight could be a display of grace and swordsmanship, or it could be a dull slaughter. That afternoon it was more likely to be the latter than the former. The first bull to appear looked shy. He had no pep. He seemed to know what was in store for him or he might have been hurt during the morning run. The crowd shouted its disapproval. The bull had to be led away out of the ring. This was done by bringing steers. For some reason the bull followed them. The next morning, as it is customary, he undoubtedly was slaughtered and his meat sold as steaks.

The next bull was more vivacious. He responded with lots of energy to the teasing of the matador. However, he obviously had not read the book, how to be a good bull in the arena, for when the time came for the picador to weaken the bull, the latter was more concerned in attacking the horse than the man on its back. Soon, he was able to pierce the padding of the horse and we saw the bloody guts of the horse as he was lifted by the powerful horns of the bull. Another picador had to come to finish that part of the bullfight. By that time my interest in bullfighting had decreased to zero. I did not pay much attention as to how that particular bull was killed by the matador. I guess he must have done allright judging by the reaction of the crowd.

I felt better a few minutes later when another bull came into the ring. He was not as energetic as the previous one. And he became weak from the teasing of the picadors and the placing of the banderilas, for when the time came for the matador to do his thing, the bull did not want to do his. He refused to fight and he had to be urged to do so. It looked more like a slaughter than a fight. The audience was screaming at the picadors, matador, and the like, throwing hats into the arena. These last two corridas were a big disappointment for every one concerned. The bullfight had ended on a sour note and we returned to our quarters with the firm conviction that bullfights were not our cup of tea. But we had a good afternoon with our friends. So not everything had been lost.

After two weeks relaxing, reading, walking along the streets and the gardens of Barcelona, of which I have little recollection, we got the expected message: to walk down to the railway station and join a convoy of about 500 people, mostly French people. Part of the group were a few women, some single, some married with children. We were going to Algeciras, at the Southern tip of Spain.

It took us many hours to get there, but we had plenty of time to swap stories, tell jokes, including some risqué ones. Morale was high. After all we were on the road to freedom. We learned that many of our companions were never put in jail, but had simply walked the 60 miles from the French border to Barcelona. They did this easily because, being from villages close to the Spanish border, they either spoke Spanish or Catalan- the dialect of the region of the Eastern Pyrenees- and therefore passed for Spanish natives. Once in Barcelona, they had gone directly to the American Consulate which helped them to stay a few days in the city and take the same train we did.

We slept on the train and it was only at the end of the next afternoon that we reached Algeciras, which was nothing but a railway terminal, a town of a few thousand people. Just across from it we saw Gibraltar, a crouching lion-like rock outline against the sky. We left the train and walked along some docks, took a barge out to a Free French boat that was waiting for us. We were deliciously happy to see at last the French flag on the top mast waving in the wind. At last, after four long years, we were free of the German presence. We climbed on the upper deck and yelled at the top of our lungs: "Vive de Gaulle!" We sang patriotic songs, then finally went below deck to eat a typical navy dinner: beans and wine. The boat sailed on to Casablanca, the biggest harbor in French Morocco.

Our Trip from Barcelona to Algeciras

PART 8

JOIN THE FRENCH AIRFORCE AND SEE THE UNITED STATES

CHAPTER 23

Casablanca

In the final choice a soldier's pack is not so heavy a burden as a prisoner's chains.

DWIGHT EISENHOWER

Usually the sea off Gibraltar is smooth as a mirror, but that day it was rough. The high ocean waves were unfurling east into the strait and as we crossed it many of us became truly sea sick. We soon discovered who among us were born sailors. Lucky me, I was. This malaise fortunately lasted only twenty minutes. At nightfall we were given blankets and told to sleep on the open upper deck, which we did. In the early morning it rained. But we were so happy that we did not care. For breakfast we had some good French bread, but nothing else. Late in the morning we reached Casablanca.

Immediately after disembarking, we were all interrogated by Allied intelligence. This was no laughing matter as we soon discovered. We were asked a lot of questions concerning our lives between 1940 and 1944, our political views, our families, and our home towns. The average interrogation lasted four hours. The Allies wanted to be sure that we were bona fide escapees and not German spies. In fact, their intelligence was so thorough that four men among us were discovered to be German and were immediately shot. Who were the four? I did not know. Had I spoken with them? I had no idea.

Trying to find whether or not I was telling the truth, an agent asked where the post office was in Menton. Was it on the right side or was it on the left side of the street that leads to the Church. I told him it was on the right. He insisted that I was wrong. It became clear to me that he had never been in my home town and was playing a game with me. It was the way I answered the question that interested him, not the answer itself. After four hours I was let go. I found Gilles at the exit of the building, happy as I was to be really free at last.

Only one thing remained for us to do: join the Allied forces. Since we were volunteering, we had the choice of the branch in which we wanted to serve. Would it be the Army, the Navy, or the Airforce? Father"s experience during World War I had taught us never to join the army if we could help it. The Army was out. I considered the navy. But it was obvious that the Airforce had the best to offer. The recruiting officer told us that there were no training facilities for airforce personnel in North Africa and that we would be sent to Canada or the United States to be trained as pilots if we could pass the physical. That was fine with us. We had a gut feeling that we did not want to pass a lot of time in North Africa. The climate was fine but there was little else to attract us in this part of the world. Besides, going to America was a dream that any young man had at that time and we could make such a trip absolutely free. Our decision was made. Gilles and I, and many of our new friends, joined the French Airforce.

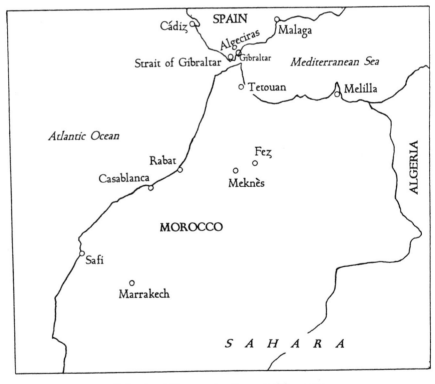

Principal Towns in French Morocco

That same night we were driven in one of the airforce bases where we were given old French uniforms that had been worn many times by others before us. It would have been an accident if they had fitted us. The pants were either too short or too long. And so were the shirts. But, the most atrocious thing we had to wear was the belt. It was big! Who on earth ever designed such a monster? Later I realized that it was the same belt the French Army had worn during World War I.

We were jealous of other French units that were comparatively well dressed. These were the original units of de Gaulle's Free French which were wearing English uniforms. Even the French Foreign Legion was better off than we were. It was obvious that we had been too late in joining the French Air Force for it was now part of the Forces of Liberation which had to scrounge for everything they needed. If we were disappointed in our uniforms, we were happy to receive some money which we did not expect. Technically, the Air Force was considering the day we crossed the Spanish border as the day of our enlistment and was paying us for those days we were in Spain. It also gave us the right to wear a small special pin that indicated that we had escaped from France. The next night we went on the town with other escapees to quietly celebrate our newly found freedom. We did this not by bar-hopping, but by walking up a small hill overlooking Casablanca. Below us was a whole city all lighted up in the night, a spectacle we had not seen for four long years.

In spite of many years of privation during the German occupation we were able to pass the qualifying physical tests of the American, French, and English Airforces. We were judged fit to fly and we were sent to another base. Part of that base was French, part American. It was easy to know which was French and which was American. G.I. Joe had a decent uniform, modern comfort, hot showers, beds with sheets. He could kill flies and mosquitoes with a new insecticide called DDT that knocked those bugs dead. G.I. Alain, on the other hand, had to sleep on a dirty straw mattress, which was infested with bed bugs and ants. He had to wash himself in cold water with a small piece of soap. G.I. Joe could go to the movies every night, but G.I. Alain was bored to death for there was little to do except play cards or listen to dirty stories.

Some of us who spoke some English decided to do something about our own comfort. We went from time to time in the American part of the base and took hot showers speaking and singing in English. The man in charge of these showers was wearing some kind of G.I. uniform and a red hat, called chechia, He was a native of Morocco and he could not tell whether we were American or French. May be, he did not care. Whatever the reason, we were never caught. To improve our English and to fight boredom in the evenings we used to jump over the wall and see American movies.

The Airforce personnel at the base was very heterogeneous. Officers and enlisted men came from all parts of France and the French Empire. There were a few like us who had recently escaped from France. Many, whose homes were in North Africa, had been drafted. Others had come from Corsica which had been liberated in late 1943. Others came from Equatorial Africa and Madagascar. Some enlisted men in our barracks were corporals or sergeants, and were obviously older and more experienced. We were not all of the same ethnic background. We were a micro-melting pot. There were all kinds of religious affiliation. Jews, Arabs, Catholics, Protestants, and non-believers. For the first time I had the chance to learn about Arab customs. One fact that intrigued me was that a young man of my age, an Arab, who was sleeping next to my bunk, had more than one wife. Though we had different backgrounds, we had one thing in common, the desire to fly.

For a month we had to learn what every trainee learns in a boot camp: discipline and the use of firearms. It was not too bad, mostly boring. We had to listen to a lot of people. We were forced, of course, to hear our officers during the day give us military instruction in such things as how to use rifles and machine guns, how to save our life in case we crashed in the Sahara desert or in the middle of the Atlantic. But the most pressing and useful advice we were to get was how to save our health, possibly our lives by not going to those famous places where one automatically gets syphilis and gonorrhea in one adventure. Some of us did not follow this wise advice and I personally saw some of the results brought about by these bacterial diseases, more dreadful then than now because we did not have antibiotics. The stories we heard in the evenings from our " sexually sophisticated" roommates were also very educational. It seemed to me that I was told about the sex life of every one on this planet. Our education in that domain became so thorough that I can say with humility that I did not learn anything new on normal or abnormal love behavior after my first two weeks of boot camp. The result of all this was that I decided that my sex life would have to wait and that the best thing for me to do in my spare time was to read some interesting books. I was certainly not the only one who came up with the same conclusion. I remember one handsome young man from Tunis who used to climb on a table and give a beautiful imitation of Mussolini telling the world that the Mediterranean sea was an Italian lake, the famous "Mare nostrum" speech. One weekend this young man, who was then a virgin, was sent to keep peace among the different branches of the service in a house of prostitution in town. He told us all the details of his education. Blushing, he added that he was still a virgin.

We were told also by our roomates more mundane but equally educational stories. The following one really impressed me:

A few months before, two young men seventeen years of age had joined the airforce. They were childhood friends who had never been away from home. They had not had the chance to adapt from a pampered home life to a more severe type of life, called bootcamp. Worse for them, they happened to be under a very inhumane drill sergeant, an adjutant, who found pleasure in terrorizing them. This reached the point that one day, these young recruits decided to kill him. But, of course they realized that the killing had to look like an accident, not like a murder. The adjutant had the habit of sneaking up on them when they were on guard duty. The young men decided to shoot him the next time he did this. In order to make it look O.K., they read the military manual carefully and devised the following scheme: when one of them was to be on guard, the other would be close by and act a witness. As soon as the adjutant approached, the one on guard would shout the regular official warning three times: "who is there? I'll shoot." But instead of timing those warnings 15 seconds apart as he was supposed to, they would be given without a time gap. What they expected happened. The adjutant sneaked up on them. One of the young men shot him, but did not kill kim, hitting him in one arm. The adjutant lost his arm and the young man who did the shooting was court-martialed. At the hearing his friend testified that the adjutant had been given the three customary official warnings, and yet had not identified himself. The young man was put in jail for two weeks and then given a two weeks leave. The adjutant retired from the airforce.

One of our duties was to guard old planes. This was strange since no one in his right mind would steal such outdated planes. It seems that in

North Africa the French Air Force and Army were more concerned with a possible revolt of the Moroccan population than a possible German attack. This threat was real, for in Morocco there has been for years a strong nationalist movement, called Istiglal, ready to strike at any moment. When France fell in 1940, the French authorities of Morocco cast their lot with the Vichy Government. But the Moroccans themselves did not. The Sultan, Mohammed V, was very cool to the Vichy Regime and stoutly opposed the adoption of its "racial" laws in his country, maintaining that the Jews of Morocco were loyal subjects who could not be discriminated against. His hopes for independence from France were raised when the Allies landed in North Africa in 1942, especially after his meeting with Franklin Roosevelt in January 1943. It was reported that during this meeting the president of the United States said to Mohammed V the following:

> *"Why does Morocco, inhabited by Moroccans, belong to France? Anything must be better than to live under French colonial rule...When we win this war, I will work with all my might to see to it that the United States is not wheeled into the position of accepting any plan that will further France's imperialistic ambitions."*

Unfortunately for Morocco, Roosevelt died before the end of the war and with him the American support for independence. No one in the U.S. raised again the Moroccan flag. And in fact, from 1943 to 1945 the Algiers government, which had supplanted the Vichy Government, continued a policy of suppression arresting many nationalists. When Gilles and I were in Casablanca, we did not know the history of Morocco, but our aim in enlisting in the Airforce had been very clear: to fight the Germans, not the natives of Morocco. I suspect that the reasons for which we had been on the side of Free France were possibly the same for which the Moroccans wanted their independence and I am not sure what would have happened if we had been given the order to fire on the Moroccan population. Fortunately, we were never confronted with this problem. Order, if not law, prevailed throughout the time we were in North Africa. And so the only times I had a loaded gun in my hands were those nights of guard duty next to these obsolete planes, parked among tall weeds at the edge of the airfield. These Moroccan nights were rather pleasant, being preferable to the days with their constant intense light, and they were quiet except for the chirping sound of the crickets.

At the time we were in Casablanca the Moroccan population was hostile not only to the French, but also to the American troops who were living in luxury, while the natives lived in complete misery. To survive, the latter were stealing from the soldiers, on base or off base. I discovered this to be true the very day of my enlistment. I was given two shirts. I washed one of them, and hung it on a clothesline inside the base. When I came back fifteen minutes later, it had disappeared.

It was extremely dangerous to go alone into the Medina, the old town. Quite a few American soldiers, in particular officers, who obviously had more money than G.I's, had ventured alone into the Medina and had been robbed and killed. In spite of these dangers, we often went into downtown Casablar :a but always in groups of at least six to eight people, trying to be as careful s possible. Even then, many of us were robbed. Our watches disappeared and were sold openly a few hours later in the streets. This was so well known that one of our friends who had his watch stolen thought that he might find it again if he went to the Place de France, the true Central Market in Casablanca. Posing as an avid buyer he described the watch he wanted. It took him only thirty six hours to find his own watch.

Casablanca is a city of two civilizations, Arab and European. On the east the Medina, the old Moroccan town, with its popular districts, swarming with merchants on the streets and in small shops, is walled in with four gates, Bab Marrakech, Bar El Kebir, Bab Sidi Beliout and Bab El Marsa. On the west lies a modern city, without any historic monuments, a model of urban planning, with its long elegant avenues linked by roundabouts. Place de France, full of vitality, is the center of Casablanca. It is overlooked by handsome buildings such as the Palais de Justice and the prefecture, whose local architecture is an eclectic marriage of Moorish, Rococo and Colonial French design. A clock tower on the top of the Prefecture building was erected by the French to teach the population the meaning of time.

Casablanca, nevertheless, like any modern metropolis, is a city with slums, called bidonville, with a reputation for extreme poverty and prostitution. Everywhere I went in Casablanca little shoeshine boys rushed down at my feet eager to shine my shoes. Though I realized that this was the only job that these entreprising shoe-shine boys could have, I refused their services. On my military pay of ten cents a day, I could not afford to have my shoes shined more than once a day.

These entreprising boys were not lazy, not like the little Arab in one of the famous stories of Alphonse Daudet which goes like this:

In a Moroccan village there was a little Arab who wanted to do as little as possible. His desperate father asked him what profession he had chosen. The son responded: "I want to be the laziest man in the village."Father: "That is impossible since there is one man who already has the job. He does absolutely nothing. The village cannot afford another one." The son: "Dad, that is my vocation."

The father finally decided to bring his son to the laziest man to see if he really was fit for the job. He found him under a fig tree. After being told about the reason of the visit, the laziest man told the young boy to lay under the fig tree. The boy stayed absolutely immobile.

From time to time a juicy succulent fig fell on the ground. If the fig was next to the laziest man he would pick it up and eat it. But the boy did absolutely nothing. After one hour, a fig fell on his cheek. He did not move. Finally, after five minutes, he could not resist any more the aroma of this enticing fig, he called his father and asked him to put the fig in his mouth.

The old man jumped to his feet and then prostrated himself in front of the boy yelling "Oh! Master. Oh! Master. Forgive me. I should never have doubted your talents. I have to resign my title. You are indeed the laziest person in the village and should be recognized as such."

A few times our unit went to the Municipal Swimming Pool which is cut in the natural rock of the shore and into which water comes directly from the ocean. I never saw such an immense pool where literally hundreds of people can go swimming at one time. One day as we walked from the airbase to the pool, a beautiful young lady was riding a horse on the left side of the avenue. The young lieutenant who was in charge that day gave us the following military order: "Head left!" All of us at unison turned our heads in the direction of the young horsewoman who blushed and rode away. Well, we were cruel, but we should be forgiven, for we are only young once as one of us, a born philosopher no doubt, used to remind us every time we complained about our military life. "Remember," he used to say, " when you will be old, you will tell your grandchildren that this was the best time of your life." He was absolutely right.

One day Gilles and I went into downtown Casablanca to the U.S.O. which was frequented by American, French, British soldiers of every type of service: infantry, airforce and navy. The main activities were dancing or eating sandwiches. Gilles and I decided to go for sandwiches. One lady, in her late thirties, asked us where our home was. The following is the shortest ensuing conversation on record:

Us: "Antibes."

The Lady: "That is very interesting. My brother lives there."

Us: "What is his name?"

The Lady:" Pouget. He is a physician."

We could not believe it. The lady who was giving us sandwiches was the sister of our home physician. Life is full of surprises. She later invited us at her home where we met her husband who was an Intelligence Officer. He volunteered to send a radio message to our parents. We chose the following words: "Alain-Gilles saw Isabel." The reader might remember that Isabel was the Spanish lady who helped Mother in the Summer of 1942. Hence, the message meant that we have crossed the Spanish border and since it was Radio Algiers which transmitted the message, our parents would be able to deduce that we were in North Africa. Our parents never heard the message, but friends of theirs heard it, understood it, and transmitted the good news to them.

Our parents did not hear from us until two weeks after the 15th of August when the Allies landed on the French Riviera and liberated our home. Though there was no regular mail as yet between North Africa and France, planes from time to time were leaving Casablanca for Southern France, and the pilot had a large white bag that all of us who had parents in France stuffed with letters.

CHAPTER 24

Rabat

And seek for truth in the groves of Academe.

HORACE

The only Moroccan town other than Casablanca that we came in contact with was Rabat, the elegant administrative capital of the French protectorate. It is a beautiful city 45 miles away from Casablanca, a matter of an hour's drive down an excellent road. If Casablanca is filled with hustle and bustle, Rabat is quiet and dignified and has a rich heritage. Originally it was built in the tenth century to oust a heretic Berber tribe who occupied the old Roman site of Sala, now known as Chellah. Two centuries later the sultan Yaccoub El Mansour decided to convert Rabat into an imperial city, building massive ramparts and gates and the great Hassan Mosque. Its successors added refined touches such as fountains and gardens.

For the next four hundred years Rabat was a haven for pirates who struck all along the Atlantic coast as far north as Ireland and as far west as the Carribean. Though piracy decreased in activity during the next two hundred years, it really disappeared only when, in 1912, the French conquered Morocco. It was then that Rabat spread beyond its ramparts. And so, like Casablanca and other Moroccan cities, Rabat has side by side crowded Moorish quarters of great antiquity, the walled-in Medina, and spacious, well planned modern districts which have grown up during the present century. This separation of two different cultures in the same city was the result of careful planning by Marshall Lyautey, the first French governor who ruled Morocco. He did not want to disturb the old Arab Medina, because, according to him, he wanted to preserve the Moroccan civilization with its old customs that he respected. Moroccan nationalists had another version. For them Lyautey did it for military reasons, it would be easier for him to put down a rebellion if the native population was living in only one restricted place. Whatever his reason was, Lyautey had a fine modern city built alongside it, complete with flower gardens, cathe-

187

dral, law courts, barracks, hospital, wide avenues lined with trees and flowering shrubs. It is there that, for the first time, I saw highways with pink oleander bushes. The next time was to be in California.

If the modern town offers all amenities, it is the old town that is interesting for its markets, its souks or small stores, for the Grand Mosque, for its middle-age fountains, for the mellah, the former Jewish quarter, with its numerous synagogues, and the Kasbah des Ouidais, which stands on the original site of the town. The Kasbah is surrounded by walls thirty feet high and nine feet thick with one superb entrance, the Bab el Kasbah, the Oudaia gate. The Kasbah has a Spanish flavor with its Andalusian village and gardens.

Before leaving France we had been told that we had distant relatives in Rabat. A couple and two children. The young lady, a painter, was a distant cousin of Mother. Her husband, a chemist by profession, was at the time a private in the army. They had two children. We decided to see them as soon as it became possible. One weekend we took the train to Rabat and went to their home. They were very glad to see us for they had no news from the rest of the family.

Though they were short of money—we knew exactly how much a private makes in the French army—a few francs a month, they offered to let us stay at their home for the weekend. We accepted the invitation on the condition that we pay for some of the food. It was possible for us to do this, for fortunately, we still had some money from home. We all had a marvelous time and Gilles and I promised we would come back, which we did more than once.

We went to Rabat another time with 25 other recruits for some military reason which I do not remember. We were to stay overnight at some barracks on the edge of town. But no one of us felt like doing this. I do not know and I don't want to know, where and how our airforce friends passed the night, but Gilles and I decided to see our cousins again and sleep the night in good beds, with white sheets, mind you. The next morning we-the twenty seven of us- met at 7.00 A.M. at the entrance of the barracks. We soon realized that we did not have a pass to get in and could not explain our re-entry on the airforce grounds. Fortunately, some enterprising genius came up with a great idea. He told us to form a column and he would take command of the column. We had no time to discuss his military leadership, the column was formed. He immediately played the role of a corporal, yelling the following marching orders: one-two, one-two. We marched so well that the sentry dropped the chain across the entry road and saluted us. Obviously he had recognized in us the best cadets that the airforce had produced.

Later, in July, we passed a whole week in Rabat. We had left France without finishing our last high school year. Wanting to graduate officially from high school, we had stipulated, as a condition of our enlistment in the airforce, that we should have a leave of absence to pass the baccalaureate. The airforce had presented no objection to our project for, at that time there was a shortage of officers and all high school graduates were potential officers, and so, anticipating our high school graduation, the airforce had already classified Gilles and I as officer cadets from the first day of our enlistment. Hence, when we approached our commanding officer, he told us that he would give us a week leave in July when such examinations were offered at Rabat. In order to be ready we borrowed books that we read from cover to cover.

Since the authorities did not have access to our school records-after all France was still under the German occupation, we had to fill out all kinds of necessary papers which had to be certified by officials at the City Hall. We went there twice—one time to bring the papers which we gave to a young lady, a second time, a week later to get them back. But, when we went back the second time, something extraordinary had happened, and undoubtedly will never happen again in the history of French bureaucracy. Our papers were not only ready but they were ready to be picked up on the desk of this young lady who apparently had been waiting for Gilles to show up. From the way she looked at him as she was giving us our papers, it was obvious, even to my inexperienced eyes, that she had a crush on my brother. What did she see in him? I have no idea. Anyway, nothing sentimental ever came out of this administrative encounter.

We passed the first week-end of July in Rabat at our cousins'home to relax before attempting to pass the baccalaureate examination. We were apprehensive, of course. After all, we were not sure that we were ready. But we thought we had to try, and Monday morning, bright and early we showed up at the lycée. We went directly to the examination room. There we were immediately struck by the fact that among the students there were young ladies in their Moroccan garb, but unveiled. Since our arrival in Morocco the only female faces we had seen belonged to French women. But that morning we were looking at the faces of young Moroccan women who were sharing with us the anxieties of taking one of the most important exams in our lives. Passing that examination was the key to a university education. These young ladies gave me my first real lesson in human multidiversity and adaptation. They were perfectly adapted to two cultures. In the Lycée, without their veils, they acted like young French women. Outside the building they veiled themselves and acted like young Moslem women.

We were given questions in mathematics, chemistry, physics and philosophy. Each set of questions had to be answered in two hours. At the end of the day we were finished with the written part of the examination. We waited two days to know the results of our efforts. Total success. We were told that we should show ourselves for the oral examination that Friday. We did and were successful. The idea that there might have been some bias in our favor in the mind of the examiners entered our mind. After all we were the only high school candidates who were in uniform and had recently escaped from France. These were not ordinary circumstances in which to pass an exam. There might have been bias during the oral examination where the examiners were face to face with us, but there could not have been for the written part of the examination, because in order to prevent any, the examiners do not know who wrote the papers. With or without some bias, Gilles and I each had our diploma and we came back to Casablanca.

Chapter 25

Waiting For Godot

Nothing happens; nobody comes; nobody goes.

SAMUEL BECKET

Passing the baccalaureate brought a let down. We did not know what to do any more to pass the time while waiting for the ship that would bring us to the New World. Every day was similar to the one before. Every day we ate omelets. Morocco is one of the largest exporter of eggs. Every day we fought flies and mosquitoes. Every day we got up at six o-clock to be at the flag raising ceremony, a very unexciting daily event. However, one morning, something special happened. It was customary that, as part of the reveillé, six of us, poor souls, had to fire a salute. That particular morning, Gilles was part of the six. At the right time he put a blank bullet in the barrel of his gun as he should. But the bullet did not fit. So he put it in his pocket and told himself that five shots would be heard as well as six shots. The officer of the day yelled "fire". But no shots were heard. He repeated his command." I said: Fire!." Still no shots were heard. Every one of the six airmen had been given machine gun bullets instead of carbine bullets. Though the six privates were not really responsible for such a fiasco, they were punished and my brother had to clean the cafeteria with a defective broom.

As we were waiting for our orders, the liberation of France, which had started on D-Day, June 6, was continuing without us. Leclerc's second motorized division entered Paris on the 27th of August. Twelve days before the American Eighth Army under the command of General Patch and the French First Army under the command of the General de Lattre de Tassigny had landed on the French Riviera, in the Maures Region between Toulon and Cannes.

Three days later Marseilles and Toulon were in the hands of the French troops. Four weeks later the whole French region east of the Rhone valley was liberated. We had hoped to hear from our parents, but we did not. Later we learned that, during the liberation of our home, they were west of the Rhone valley in a village of the Massif Central which was liberated later by Scottish paratroopers. According to Mother it was one of the most striking events in her life to see them slowly landing at her feet. Freedom was coming from the sky. It took my parents days, bicycling part way, part way getting rides on military vehicles to go back to Antibes.

Thirty-eight years later my wife, whose maiden name is McLennan, and I were in Inverness, Scotland. We were having lunch with the chief of the McLennan clan, who told me that he had been in France in 1944 when he was a paratrooper. He could not remember the place, but it was in the mountains in the center of France. The reader can guess: Ronald McLennan was one of the paratroopers who landed at my parents' feet. In their names I thanked him and his friends for having given so much joy to them that September in 1944.

The next few months, the Airforce attempted to entertain us by teaching us the Morse code, how to recognize allied and enemy planes, and by giving us our first flying lessons aboard a mechanical cockpit, called "link trainer", which had all the instruments and controls of a real airplane. I was told I could do everything that I would do in a regular airplane except to take off and crash. In my case it was a good thing, for the first time I was asked to take the controls of the link trainer I went 2,000 feet underground. This was not promising, but I was forgiven. After all there was no actual damage to the plane.

During the occupation of France, I did not, as many other young Frenchmen, have an opportunity to go to concert halls and enjoy classical music or operas of any kind. My experience in hearing music was restricted to listening without any real enthusiasm to records that Father used to play on a phonograph or to radio broadcasts from Radio-Monte Carlo. It was in Casablanca that I had my first taste of an opera. I owed this opportunity to Corporal Jean Durizy, a young man who could sing, dance, tell jokes and enchant women. I could not do any of these things, and yet for some obscure reason, we became friends. Well, one day he asked me to go with him to hear the French opera Carmen by Georges Bizet. I accepted his invitation because I thought it would be nice to go with him and see something new. The fact that I had played marbles in the streets of Menton with Bizet's grandson might also have had something to do with my desire to see Carmen. In any event, we passed a Saturday afternoon in the local amphitheater. I was not thrilled, may be because the tenor who represented Don Jose was fifty years old and very fat, and that the mezzo-soprano who sang Carmen was not much better. My first encounter with opera was a big disappointment, but only a temporary one, for I discovered later that among the pleasures of my life hearing operas was high on the list. I found that I like some operas better than others. The ones I like have to have both pleasant music and interesting stories. And Carmen, the first opera I heard in Casablanca, is one of them.

During the month of September, we got hope that maybe soon we would be going to the United States after all. The sixteenth detachment to be trained in America left us. Gilles and I were part of the seventeenth. If the Airforce command were logical, we should be next on the list. These detachments were made up of about 150 enlisted men commanded by a captain and two lieutenants. The enlisted men's rank ranged from private to the equivalent of master sergeant. All of us were to be trained as flying personnel on American planes, for France had no planes of her own. As graduates from flying school, we would be wearing our airforce wings on our chest. However, contrary to what happens in the United States Airforce, where when a student pilot graduated from flying school he is automatically promoted to a second lieutenant, in the French Airforce a new pilot with the rank of private is promoted either to a sous-lieutenant (second lieutenant) or sergeant depending on his education. Those with a high school diploma were promoted to second lieutenant unless, of course, they were already a lieutenant, a captain or a major and in that case they obviously kept their rank or were promoted to the next one. The new pilot who had not graduated from high school was promoted to sergeant unless he had already a higher rank.

Only very few of the men to be trained as flying personnel in he U.S., officers or enlisted men, had experience as pilots, bombardiers, or gunners either in the French or the Royal Air forces. They were permitted of course to wear the corresponding wings.

Later, when we were in the States, one of us who had just graduated from pilot school put on his chest his newly acquired American wings, his Royal Air force wings, and his French Force wings. He was very proud until one of his friends remarked aloud that he could do as well or even better, for he could add, he said, the Luftwaffe wings. We asked if he were kidding. He said no and he explained that as an Alsatian he was drafted in the German Air force and taught how to fly. The first day that he flew solo he went directly to London. But, in order to prevent his German plane from being shot by the British antiaircraft guns, he continuously spoke in French on the radio from the minute he flew over the Channel. He landed without any problem and the next day he was flying a British plane.

Chapter 26

Oran, Off To The States

The town itself, let us admit, is ugly. It has a smug, placid air and you need time to discover what it is that makes it different from so many business centers in other parts of the world. How to conjure up a picture, for instance, of a town without pigeons, without trees or gardens, where you never hear the beat of wings or the rustle of leaves-a thoroughly negative place, in short?

ALBERT CAMUS
Describing Oran in The Plague.

Finally we got our orders to depart for the United States. The seventeenth detachment was on its way to Oran, Algeria. Off hand it did not make sense to go east instead of west to America. But of course Columbus went west from Spain to go to India. However, from a military point of view this trip to Oran might make sense for we had to travel on U.S. ships and those ships which were in the Mediterranean sea were going back and forth to Italy. They had no business coming to Casablanca to pick up 150 French souls who wanted to fly. The chances were far better that a friendly captain of an American ship returning to the States, stopping in Oran, would find it in his heart to bring us to his own country.

We were asked if some of us knew how to drive cars. A few answered in the affirmative and were immediately volunteered to drive trucks over the Atlas mountains to Oran. The rest of us took the train for Algeria. Though the distance between Casablanca and Oran is about 500 miles it took us two days to get there, for the train stopped not only at the important cities of Fez, Meknes, Taourirt, Oudjda, Lalla Marnja, Tlemcen and Sidi Bel Abbes, but a lot of places in the middle of nowhere. Many of our Moroccan and Algerian friends were very happy that the train stopped in their home town for it gave their families the chance to see them and then bid good bye before they left for the States. After all they had no idea when they would be back home. Those of us who were from metropolitan France felt left out.

Comfort on the train was at a minimum. We sat and slept on wooden benches. We ate bread and a lot of sardines out of cans. But the morale was high. We knew we would be together for months. (In fact some of us would come back to France together a year later). We started to learn about each other by sharing stories and jokes. We arrived in Oran and stayed there for two boring weeks. We had nothing to do and we were in the worst material conditions we had ever been in during our military life. Hygiene was deplorable. There were no showers. Toilets were non-existent. When nature called, we had to go out in an open field behind temporary barracks which were perched on the top of the plateau overhanging the town.

Oran forms an amphitheater on the slopes of a ravine that cuts the plateau of Karguentua, which is about three hundred feet high. It is hard to find a town whose streets are so steep. In the summer, when it is hot, it is a painful climb from the harbor up to the plateau where the new town is spreading. Fortunately, street cars permit one to travel easily around the three distinct districts of Oran, the harbor and its maritime commercial facilities at the bottom of the hill, the old town clinging on the side of the hill, and the modern town on the top of the hill.

These three districts reflect, in part, the history of Oran, an original and individualistic city where the turbulence of modern life has not choked the past. The town was founded by Andalusian sailors in 902, but did not play an important role for four hundred years, since it remained under attack from tribes coming from the southern lands and from pirates. In 1509 it was conquered by the Spanish and remained under the Spanish crown for three hundred years except for a short period of 24 years when it was under the Turks. It is only since 1831 that Oran has been French. This explains why the majority of the people living in Oran are ethnically Spanish. They have kept their customs and their language.

We were sharing our quarters with soldiers also in transit waiting to go somewhere else, people whom we would never see again. However, by a fluke, I saw one of them years later. I was on my way to a skiing station near Briancon. As I was taking a bus, I saw a young man whose face I thought I recognized. He also thought he had seen me before. But neither he nor I could remember where. It took us three minutes to solve this problem. He was the soldier on the bunk above mine in these awful barracks on the top of the hill in Oran.

To keep clean Gilles and I decided to go downtown to the public baths. We did not mind paying a few francs, for we thoroughly enjoyed getting into a bathtub and scrubbing ourselves. I do not know if it is still true now, but then water was scarce in Oran and the drinking water was very salty. This became very obvious to us when one day in a cafe we ordered minted drinks, and to our astonishment even those drinks were salty. We could not wait to leave Oran.

Finally the day of embarkation came, and we were to board a U.S. boat which had anchored in the bay of Mers-el-Kebir a few miles from Oran. Big ships cannot enter Oran harbor because it is too small and too shallow. On the contrary, the deep bay of Mers-el-Kebir, because of its location protected from the winds coming from every direction, has been a natural haven for navies of every kind for centuries. It was in this bay that part of the French navy took refuge after the armistice, and was in the fall of 1940 destroyed or sunk by the English who were afraid that the French navy would fall in the hands of Hitler. More than 2,500 sailors were killed or wounded. This action could have been prevented if cooler heads had prevailed. The English had given the French Admiral three choices. The first choice was to join the English navy in its battle against Hitler. The second choice was to sail into neutral harbors, preferably in the States. The third choice was to be sunk by the more powerful guns of the Royal Navy anchored a mile away. The French Admiral would not accept the first choice because there was a deep rivalry between the two navies. He never considered the second choice. So four hours after receiving the English ultimatum the French Admiral saw his ships destroyed.

With very few personal belongings, we, the members of the seventeenth detachment, the future backbone of the French Airforce, got into a large motor boat which brought us in to Mers-el-Kebir Bay to board the ship that was to carry us across the Atlantic. The boat was returning to the States empty. Except for the crew we were the only Allied soldiers on board. To our astonishment we found on board very close to a hundred seriously wounded German soldiers who were to be treated in the States. We thought that this was very generous on the part of the United States to treat her enemy in that fashion.

We were part of a convoy of ten ships that immediately departed. A mine sweeper was continuously passing back and forth in front of the convoy whose sides were protected by two destroyers. Under these conditions it was not astonishing that it took us eleven days to cross the Atlantic. Though the trip was very slow, it was a safe one and we enjoyed it very much, in great part because the food was excellent: lots of steaks and French fries. I gained 11 pounds in those 11 days. This was a good thing for my weight was only 110 pounds when I left Oran.

We were given jobs to do during our trip. We had a choice between painting the decks or feeding the wounded German prisoners. Gilles and I volunteered to carry food trays from the kitchen to the beds of the German prisoners in a makeshift infirmary three times a day. It was an easy job, but one morning an incident occurred. We were serving breakfast to the Germans in beds. The boat rolled and one of us dumped some hot coffee on the sheets of one German, burning him slightly. The German swore to the French "waiter," who happened to be an Alsatian speaking German fluently. Mad as hell, our friend told the German soldier that his brother was a prisoner in a German camp and was not served breakfast in bed. He promptly dumped the whole tray on the bed. Someone cleaned up the mess, but it was not one of us.

We arrived in New York November 7, 1944, the very day Franklin Roosevelt was elected for the fourth time President of the US. Our escape from occupied France had been a total success. We were now ready to turn a page in our lives, hoping to reach our goal of fighting the Germans by becoming aviators.

EPILOGUE

EPILOGUE

Gilles and I had joined the Allied Forces in North Africa to fight against the Germans, but we never did. When the war in Europe ended in April 1945, we were still in the United States. A few weeks later Gilles got his pilot wings, but I never did. My depth perception was so bad that I was never allowed to start my pilot training. Instead I became a clerk and an interpreter at Gunterfield, an airforce base near Montgomery, Alabama. Since the war against Japan continued, the French Air Force was to help liberate French Indochina. But before we had the chance to pack up, the atomic bomb exploded in August 1945 and we were told that we could become civilians again. Father, the antimilitarist, sent us two telegrams to be sure we got the message.

Gilles decided that he wanted to study engineering in the United States and he was discharged in Washington. He then came to Michigan where he got his Ph.D in 1952 in the field of mechanical engineering and, after working for a while for Douglas Aircraft, he became a Professor of mechanical engineering at the University of California at Berkeley. He retired in 1990. He is now busy building dams and bringing drinking water to villages in Central and South America. He is also the founder and chairman of a new company that deals with fiber optics switches. You can find him relaxing high in the French Alps where he has a home. He continues to climb mountains and ski.

I went back to France, was discharged in Paris in November 1945, and took over the family farm at Roquebrune. I worked very hard at Clair Matin for two years, but Father and I did not make much of a profit. The primitive agricultural practices on the French Riviera caused me to consider going back to the United States to study easier methods of plant cultivation. So, in November 1947, I went to California and I enrolled as a special horticulture student at California State Polytechnic College, at San Luis Obispo. A few weeks later I was advised by an instructor, Howard Brown, who later became a personal friend, to take a degree in Horticulture, which I obtained in 1950. I then moved to East Lansing, Michigan, to do graduate work in botany and agronomy at Michigan State College, now Michigan State University. In March 1952, I became a U.S. citizen. In June of that year I got my Master's degree in Botany and Plant Pathology. After getting my

Ph.D.in agronomy in 1958 I went to work as a plant breeder in California and three years later I became a biology teacher, first at the University of California at Santa Barbara, then at the Oregon College of Education at Monmouth. Then I moved to my Alma Mater where for a number of years I taught science to non-scientists and had the chance to do research in my first love, plant biology. I retired from teaching in 1991.

When it became obvious to our parents that Gilles and I had settled in the United States, they immigrated to this country in 1950. They passed the last years of their lives around San Francisco. Father died in 1960 at the age of 76 when, according to medical prediction, he should have died a long time before of kidney troubles caused by war injuries that he suffered during World War I. Mother died in 1980 at the ripe age of 88, after volunteering for years at the Children Hospital of Oakland.

The last few years of my professional life, I became interested in the history of biology, in particular the history of genetics and the life and work of Gregor Mendel. My going from the history of science to the history of World War II seems to have been an easy step. It looks like the story of my escape from France was left on the back burner, and as soon as I had retired I wrote it.

The reader might ask the question, did I regret leaving my beloved Provence in 1947? Not really, because at that time, I thought I was coming back to France after my studies in the States. Looking back now, I do not regret passing my adult life in the U.S. instead on the Riviera. I had the chance to visit the homestead once more in 1978 and though, according to my American wife, I was very excited, I had no problem coming back to the States, having become more American than French. In addition, the French Riviera has changed very much, and not for the best. Though it is still beautiful in many ways, it has become too touristic, with too many people, too many houses, and too much pollution. If there is a French region in which I would love to have a home, it is the Brianconnais. I had the chance to see it again in 1984 and 1986. It has kept all its charm. It was during my 1984 visit that I saw Madame Rousset, the widow of our physical education instructor at Briancon High School who taught us not only gymnastics, but mountain climbing as well. She told me a few fascinating stories about the liberation of the region in 1944. Wanting to know more I promised her to come back and recapture her memories on tape, which I did two years later. I have included them in the next and last chapter of this book.

PART 9

THE LIBERATION OF THE BRIANÇONNAIS

Chapter 27

The Liberation Of The Briançonnais
Madame Rousset's eyewitness account

We fight not to enslave, but to set a country free, and to make room upon the earth for honest men to live in.

THOMAS PAINE

The liberation of Southern France occurred in August 1944 when Gilles and I were still in French Morocco, waiting transfer to the United States to be trained as pilots. We did not participate in the liberation of our home country, though obviously we would have loved to do so. On August 15, 1944, United States and French troops landed with little trouble on the south coast of France, between Cannes and Toulon. The French were given the task of liberating Toulon and Marseilles which they did successfully on August 28, freeing the whole French Riviera of the German presence. However, Menton and Roquebrune were liberated by Japanese-American troops who came through Italy.

The Americans went immediately up the Rhone valley, and in less than four weeks after the southern landing linked up with Patton's Third Army. They liberated Grenoble on the 20th of August, and some of their motorized elements were sent south up the Romanche valley through the Lauteret pass and down the Guisane valley to liberate Briançon. While the liberation of the French Riviera was accomplished very rapidly, the liberation of Briançon was a very tough and painful job. I learned this years later from an excellent witness, Madame Marguerite Rousset.

In the Summer of 1984 my wife, Joanne, and I were travelling by car from Grenoble to Aix in Provence and stopped in the village of Le Monetier. I wanted to see again this alpine village where, during 1943 and early 1944, Gilles and I met on weekends our parents who had taken refuge from the Nazis. I had fond memories of this village, for it is there that we were fed for the week as there was so little food to eat in the high school cafeteria, and this is where, in spite of the warlike conditions we had so much fun skiing.

I found the village changed much physically. It is now a ski resort with three lifts. There was none in the 40's. Half the village is new, with modern homes, shops, and new hotels. The other half is still the way I remember: the old houses with their thick cemented walls and their narrow and heavy doors, the narrow streets which are now cleaner than they used to be and water still running in a canal in the middle of main street. The water comes from an underground hot spring and is always hot even in the coldest winter months.

We parked the car next to the old church and my wife and I went to find two ladies dear to my heart, Madame Robert and Madame Rousset, both now in their 70's. I will always be grateful to Madame Robert for the many meals she fed us between 1942 and 1944. Her gratin dauphinois with all the trimmings is still present in my memory. She was happy to see me after so many years. The hotel her husband owned now is in the hands of her eldest daughter and her son-in law. It has been modernized and the food is excellent. We talked to Madame Robert for a while and then we went to see whether Madame Rousset was home. She was. We found her incredibly physically fit and mentally alert. We talked for a few hours remembering the hard war years. Then, my wife and I left Le Monêtier, but not before I promised Madame Rousset that I would be back to capture on tape her memories of the events that preceded and happened during the liberation of the region. I came back in 1986 and the following stories are the ones she told me those three summer days we passed with her and her sister, Fernande.

To help the reader understand and appreciate Madame Rousset's stories I would like to recap the history of Briancon and its surroundings under the Axis occupation. Briançon was occupied by the Italians November 11, 1942, two days after the American troops landed in North Africa. The French military resistance was soon born and by March 1943 the first maquis or hidden camp of the French fighting forces was established high in the mountains in the vicinity of Lus la Croix Haute. Others followed at Freissinières, Pommet, the Carabes and the Lauteret passes and other locations. The first men who joined the maquis were the military personnel of the Armistice Army which was dissolved in November 1942. They were joined by escaped war prisoners, people hunted down for any political or religious reason, and young men who did not want to be sent to Germany as slave laborers. There were three different resistant groups which later united under the common name, the French Forces of the Interior, or for short F.F.I: the Secret Army, the Army Resistance Organization, and the Franc-tireurs- French partisans. On July 1943 they totaled only about 300 men, but by 15 August 1944, they were more than 3200 officers and soldiers.

At first they fought the O.V.R.A., the Italian police that corresponded to the German Gestapo, and special Italian troops. Then they fought the S.S. and German troops that had replaced the Italian troops when Italy switched sides after having been defeated by the Allies in the Summer of 1943. In September of that year, the Gestapo moved to Gap, the administrative center of the Hautes Alpes, then to Briançon. The presence of the German troops, the loss of personal freedom, the censorship of newspapers and personal letters, the severe restrictions on food and transportation affected everyone. These conditions, and the likely possibility that any young man could be deported any time to Germany to work in war factories, led most of the French population to think about only one thing: liberation from the enemy.

Interestingly, the French underground who had fought the Italian soldiers in France until the summer of 1943, helped them to return to Italy soon after. The Germans had closed the French-Italian border, giving the Italian soldiers, their former comrades-in arms, only these two choices, either continue the war against the Anglo-Americans, or be deported to Germany. Many of these soldiers attempted to go back home through the mountains. Some succeeded after having been helped by French mountainers, such as our friend Robert Rousset who knew every mountainous path as well as he did the streets of his home town.

Obviously fighting the German troops that now occupied the Hautes Alpes was far harder than fighting the Italian troops who never had the heart to fight anyone. The F.F.I. started a series of sabotages. They succeeded in destroying the aluminum factory of L'Argentiere in November and December 1943. The first attack on the railway came in February 1944 when eight train engines were blown up at Veynes. Such attacks on railway equipment intensified after D-Day. Railway tracks were entirely destroyed, preventing trains operating for a while. Then the F.F.I. became bolder and attacked German troops who in turn indiscriminately burnt villages and shot soldiers and civilians. The F.F.I were able to get the guns and ammunition they needed from three different sources: the stockpiles of the Armistice Army, the Italian stockpiles left when the Italian army fled the region, and supplies dropped by parachute which started in March 1944. Obtaining food did not present any problem because the region was and still is mostly agricultural. The farmers supplied the F.F.I. abundantly with bread, milk, and potatoes, and meat of some kind or another.

ARMED RESISTANCE IN THE BRIANÇONNAIS
(in the form of stories as told to me by Madame Rousset)

If the reader is wondering why I changed the format of the book in this chapter, it is because I wanted to record the stories just the way Madame Rousset told them to me. I was touched by these stories and I hope the reader will be also.

Italicized words, sentences or paragraphs have been added as explanations, corrections, additions to help the reader understand and appreciate more fully Madame Rousset's stories.

In the Summer of 1944 Allied agents were parachuted into places in the Alps. Their mission was to train the French Forces of the Interior to assist a specific Allied landing on the French Riviera. To reach their specific destination, they were to pass through very high mountain passes carrying their radios and necessary equipment. The task of the Resistance fighters was to pick them up at the sites where they had parachuted and to take care of them until they reached their destination. Many were to pass through the Briançonnais and the specific task of Monsieur and Madame Rousset and their friends was to be sure that they safely crossed the mountain passes overlooking Le Monêtier. This is how Madame Rousset described this task to me.

Madame Rousset. The agents who were two days before in the streets of Algiers were now with us. They had been parachuted generally at sunset in the vicinity of Serres (a town in the Basses Alpes, the department south of the Hautes Alpes where Briançon is located). They had been hidden in hay carts until they reached the base of the mountain pass. From then on, guided by expert French volunteers, they had to climb up steep mountainous paths. Their heaviest equipment was carried by mules. Most of these men had never been trained to be mountain climbers. Furthermore, they did not have the right shoes. As they tried walking in hay fields that had not been cut for years, they slid backwards and we had to help them all the way. Within a few hours most of these men were completely exhausted. It was awful.

One thing I have to say. They were, otherwise, well organized. They knew their mission and how to use their equipment, radios and guns. On the other hand, the resistance knew exactly at what time drops occurred and how to pick up those agents. These operations were highly successful and no one ever squealed to the Germans.

I will never forget one Canadian major who was big as an ox, all sweaty, who was so tired that he could not put one foot in front of the other. We carried him up the mountain pass and down until we reached a small house where we finally let him sleep in a hay stack close to the house. The next morning we could not find him. During the night he had fallen at the bottom of the hay. He slept there for twenty four hours. Though he ate very little when he woke up— we had only some sour cream and half raw potatoes to give him— he was ready to continue his journey. We had another problem with him. Though he was Canadian, he did not speak a word of French. Fortunately, he knew where he was supposed to go and to help him to find his way he used small compasses sewn on his coat instead of buttons.

The next agents we helped were English—they had the English type (sic). They had two mules which carried two big suitcases.

Alain C. (laughing.) This, I would like to have seen.

Madame Rousset. Like the other agents they were completely exhausted and we had to help them all the way. It was rough for we had to travel during the night. We could not afford to be seen during daytime by the Germans or their lackeys, because the Gestapo had placarded that anyone who specifically helped allied agents would be shot immediately.

Alain C. This must have been just before the landing on the French Riviera.

Madame Rousset. Exactly two days before. For as soon as the Englishmen arrived on the top of the mountain pass, they opened one of the suitcases which contained a powerful radio and listened for messages. I asked one of them who spoke very good French when, for heavens'sake, the landing would occur. He answered: "Madame, it is imminent. The parachutage that you expect will not occur. It is already too late." He was right, these were the last agents we helped crossing these mountain passes. The approximate date of the landing was the only secret I ever knew, for my job had been to feed these agents and take care of their health, not to know the objective of military missions. That was Robert's role, not mine.

I tell you, Alain, it was rough going, for the Germans had been enraged against the French since June 18, 1944. That day de Gaulle called on the Resistance to show the Germans that the French were ready to fight them, that they were still their enemies. The Resistance drew plans, called Fire Plans, to do exactly that.

Do you know, Alain, where we, the Resisters, met to discuss our plans?

Alain C. Not really.

Madame Rousset. Our headquarters were the old convent here in town, between the Church and the old butcher's shop.

Alain C. The one of Mr. Brun? *Mr. Brun was the man who used to sell my mother pork chops, for a price of course.*

Madame Rousset. Yes. The convent had underground passages. We met in a basement that we had to reach by climbing down a ladder. We were untroubled during our meetings which were attended by my husband and me, Mr. Robert, Mr. Brun and the former mayor of the Monétier. Incidentally, it would be useless to talk to him for this old man is now sick and has lost his memory.

Alain C. What you tell me is a clue to a mystery, to something that my father said during the winter of 1944. My parents were in a small apartment owned by Mr. Brun. A very cold evening Father saw Mr. Robert and Mr. Brun, both shivering, coming out from some building and going obviously to warm up at the hotel. Father said to us that "I just saw Mr. Brun and Mr.Robert. They acted very strangely and I wonder where they came from in the middle of the night." Now, I know. They were meeting in the old convent.

Madame Rousset. You must be right. Well, the day after de Gaulle called for action, a man came to see Robert. I think he was a major in the Secret

Army and he told Robert: "We have received the order for a fire plan. We have decided to make a guerilla attack to be held on the road to the Lauteret pass just north of Le Monétier." Robert answered him: "Absolutely not. I cannot let you do this. The population of the village is very quiet and I do not want any reprisal." The major said: "That's O.K., we have another plan. We will attack them at the road tunnel des Ardoisiers at the Galerie du Rif Blanc which is a mile from the Lauteret pass. Alain, you must remember that at that time in order to go up and down the valley we had to pass both ways up and down under the tunnel. Now, a road going down passes outside the tunnel.

Alain C. Yes, I remember.

Madame Rousset. The major asked Robert to protect him and one resistant fighter when they would blow up German trucks. Robert agreed and we notified the Resisters of Le Monetier and Le Casset that the first true day of battle, had finally come and that they were to be ready that night with their weapons. The weapons had been given to them a few months before and they had kept them religiously clean and in good order. Robert and his friends took off during the night about nine-o clock and climbed up to the tunnel of the Rif Blanc. When they arrived, they saw several German trucks, going down the Lauteret pass. When the trucks passed into the tunnel, the French major and his aide detonated an explosive blowing up the first truck. The explosion killed the major's aide instantly, but did not injure the major. What did the Germans then do? I am not sure. But I know that they stowed the trailer of the first truck on the side of the road and transferred the dead and wounded soldiers onto the second truck.

Alain C. In the night!

Madame Rousset. Yes, in the night. The trucks continued to roll down the road. Soon they would be driving across Le Monetier. Well, you imagine, Alain, how scared we were. What would be the German reaction to our guerilla act?. What would the Germans do to us if they found any of us in the streets. They certainly would shoot us down. So we (about ten people) thought it was best to hide in a garden with high walls. One of us, lying flat on his stomach on the side of the small brook just north of the village, listened to the night noises. Soon he ran to us and said: "Be careful, I heard a truck."

The first truck passed through the village without its lights, its engine not running, coasting. The main road through Le Monétier is slightly sloping.

Alain C. The Germans were as scared as you were.

Madame Rousset. We thought the other German trucks would stop and we became really scared. We were six or seven in that garden and we thought it more prudent to hide behind a bigger wall. My husband helped me to go over it. Though all of us landed in a bed of stinging nettles, no one uttered a sound. Our mind was set on more important things such as survival. Well, like the first one, the other German trucks did not stop. They coasted through the village very slowly without lights. I don't know how many trucks there were, for it was pitch dark, but I know that there were more than three. What a night! I will never forget it. The damaged first truck remained in the tunnel for a few days, as a reminder of the activity of French partisans.

From that day on, the Germans became really vicious, thinking only about reprisals against the French population. The German High Command decided to eliminate all the hard core of resistance from Briançon to the Vercors, because they believed that all the attacks came from the Vercors. *(The Vercors is a plateau in Savoy where hundreds of French Resistance fighters who did not have enough guns and ammunition were killed by well equipped German soldiers.)* A few days later a German column was sent through the valley of La Guisane and another through the valley of La Romanche. Both columns were to join north of the Lauteret pass.

We were warned first that buses crammed with German soldiers had arrived at Gap, then that they were coming through the Durance Valley, and that they had arrived at Briançon. *Most of the information concerning the movement of the German troops were obtained through a telephone operator at the town of Agnières. Her name was Odelay. She and her husband, were both members of the underground. Mr. Odelay who was a telephone lineman connected an extra line to two main telephone lines, Gap-Veynes and Gap-Grenoble, used by the Kommandantur at*

Gap. This secondary line led directly to his wife's office. Madame Odelay who was Alsatian and spoke fluently German intercepted and recorded all the conversations that the German Army officers had.

Alain C. When exactly did this cleaning- up operation by the Germans occur?

Madame Rousset. In the month of July . (In fact, It was the first week of August)

Alain C. Before the landing on the French Riviera.

Madame Rousset. Yes. Because the telephone was out by that time, we were warned that they were coming through our valley by two or three cyclists . Every one all through the valley was advised to remain inside his or her house with the shutters closed. One hour later we saw the expected busses crammed with German and Russian soldiers with sub-machine guns.

Alain C. Russian soldiers?

Madame Rousset. They were prisoners whom the Germans had made on the Russian battlefront. *(In fact they were mongols who had been drafted into the German army and who were used in all kinds of capacities.)* The busses went through Le Monétier without stopping. We were watching behind the shutters, were very scared and very quiet. All the Resistant fighters who had been alerted of the coming of the Germans were hiding along the road behind crags with fieldglasses. Unfortunately, near the Lauteret pass, the Germans picked up a few men who were in the open. One of them was a man Robert had warned of the immediate arrival of the Germans, advising him to stay inside his house. But foolishly he had discarded Robert's advice and continued with the help of his son to mow his hay field. With both the father and the son other hostages were shot a few hours later. I do not know exactly how many of these men the Germans shot near the pass. *(The exact number was 17 and the date of their execution was August 9).* But we shall see, for I will bring you there tomorrow if you like. There is now a small chapel built to their memory.

Alain C. I'd love to. (We did)

Madame Rousset. After shooting these guys, the Germans continued their drive down the pass. Worrying that the tunnels next to the pass were mined, they put the Mongol soldiers in front of them and in front of the Mongol soldiers they put several Frenchmen whom they picked up at Villard d'Arenne.

Alain C. This makes sense. They would be blown up instead of the German troops.

Madame Rousset. Exactly. In fact there was an explosion and two of the Frenchmen died. At the village of La Grave the Germans made a real rumpus. They entered homes carrying their submachine guns, raping women, scaring the hell out of old women who were crossing themselves and praying, their crucifixes in their hands. After that they descended the valley to Bourg d'Oisans where they continued their rumpus.

There, the Germans had to decide what to do with all the Frenchmen that they had rounded up.. Just kill them or release them. A major in the Wermacht, more humane than the rest of his comrades, decided that, if these men had children, they should be released. So he asked them how many they had. The answer that he got was predictable. Every man answered that he had a lot of kids, including a priest in the group who answered that he had five children.

Alain C. To save one's life one would admit to anything.

Madame Rousset. The Germans were also very wild in Briançon. But I do not know the details. Today, it is very hard to find anyone who was a witness of the events that occurred in the Summer of 1944. Some are dead. Some have disappeared. For example, there were a lot of Alsatians in the F.F.I. around here. But they all went home after the war. A few came back here to see their friends but only for a few days. By now I have lost track of them. I talked a lot with Colonel Terasson-Duvernon, however he did not fight at Briançon, but in the Queyras.

Alain C. I understand that he played an important role in the liberation of the Hautes Alpes.

Madame Rousset. When I see him next time, I will ask him to tell me the details of the burial of the American aviator.

Alain C. Oh, yes. It would be very interesting. *But in fact, I did not get the details of the burial of this American pilot, named Dudley Taylor, and whose plane crashed in flames August 15 near Lus La Croix Haute. All I know is that the whole population of the village attended his solemn funeral with military honors. They even played Taps. Where did they get the music, I don't know. This amazing funeral was carried out without the knowledge of the Germans who were a few miles away. It shows that a whole village can be united in expressing a common feeling of sympathy towards a man they did not even know.*

Madame Rousset told me two more amazing stories which took place before the liberation of Briançon. One concerns one of her friends, a civil engineer and the other her own husband.

Madame Rousset. From time to time it was necessary to find out whether the Germans were in the valleys of La Guisane and La Romanche and, if they were, what they were up to. This was a job well suited for a friend of ours, an officer of the Secret Army and a civil engineer, whose formal duty was periodically to check the local roads for safety.

One day as he was at the base of the Galibier pass, he was arrested by a German patrol whose chief rightly assumed that he was a member of the Resistance and decided that he was to be executed as soon as possible. With some other Frenchmen our friend was led to the edge of a rocky precipice and German soldiers across the road were given the order to shoot them down. At this precise moment an incredible thought went through the mind of our friend: "As long as I am going to be killed this way, I might as well try something to save my life how ever improbable this might be." As the Germans were aiming, within a second he bent backwards and made a looping (Madame Rousset used the word looping) and fell down on the rocks below. He was never hit by any bullet, but according to him he psychosomatically felt them through his body.

Though not having been hit by bullets, he was bleeding profusely from cuts and bruises resulting from his fall against the rocks. The Germans thought they had killed him on the spot and never checked if he really were dead. Our friend laid down motionless at the bottom of the precipice for at least two hours. He stayed around Le Galibier pass for two days to recuperate from wounds and shock. He drank some water from the river but had nothing to eat. The evening of the second day he went down the valley and soon he was on the threshold of our home where we saw him, haggard and saying to Robert: "Touch me, Rousset, touch me. Am I alive or dead? Am I alive or dead? Am I dreaming?" When he told us his story, we easily understood why the poor man was so disturbed.

In order to take care of his wounds, we undressed him. His shoulders were a mess. They were very red and terribly scratched.

Alain C. Had he a fever?

Madame Rousset. Not really, but he was in bad shape. He was alive. That was the important thing. We comforted him. We gave him drink and food. A few hours later he was on his way to Briançon. Somewhere it was written that it was too early for him to die.

Alain C. He was a fast thinker and courageous man. Is he still alive?

Madame Rousset. Oh yes! I learned that he is now retired.

Alain C. You promised to tell me another story about what happened to your husband when he was up in the mountains.

Madame Rousset. Oh! yes. One day Robert decided to see what was going on the North side of the Galibier. He climbed over the pass and started going down through some pasture lands dotted with old chalets. This Summer of 1944, no one was around, for the region had become a small battlefield between the Germans and the Forces of the Underground. As Robert was inside one of these chalets looking through his fieldglasses, he heard a terrible commotion, as if someone had jumped onto the corrugated iron roof, an easy thing to do for anyone because of the steepness of the hillside. Robert who obviously could not see who jumped on the roof had only one thought: "It must be some German soldiers who were hiding and I am done for." He waited, but no one came.

Finally, not hearing any more noise, he decided to investigate. What he saw on the roof was a lost goat munching some grass along the edge of the roof and looking at him as though she was asking what is the matter with you, you are shaking like a leaf.

Alain C. What a relief!

Madame Rousset. You bet! But Robert did not come back empty handed. He brought us a whole wheel of cheese that the farmers, owners of the chalet, had left when they fled. Alain, I still remember this delicious cheese. What a feast!

LIBERATION OF BRIANÇON.

The liberation of Briançon which started the 24th of August proved to be a very tough and a very painful job. This is how Madame Rousset described it to me.

Madame Rousset. We heard a car that was going down the road from the Lauteret pass. It was the 23rd of August. Robert decided to investigate, for if this car were a German car there might be trouble for his many friends who were hidden close by. Standing behind a rock he looked through his field glasses and he came to the conclusion that the car did not look like either a German or a French car. There were four men in it with helmets and carbines. The idea that they could be American soldiers was so preposterous that for a few moments he stood there stunned. But, in fact, right in front of him, there were indeed four American G.I.s in a jeep, all by themselves. Robert finally stopped the jeep that was going very slowly, introduced himself as a member of the Secret Army. Robert did not know English and the Americans did not know French, which limited their conversation a lot.

Alain C. Too bad I was not there.

Madame Rousset. That is true.

Alain C. What was the military rank of your husband?

Madame Rousset. I really don't know. I think he was a warrant officer. But he could have been a second lieutenant. Whatever he was, they all embraced and Robert brought them to Le Monétier where the whole population, kids and adults, went wild offering the Americans champagne and who knows what. The G.I.s decided to continue their trip to Briançon. And Robert decided to accompany them. He told me so and jumped in the jeep. They took off.

Alain C. There were only four G.I.s and Robert. Only five men going down to Briançon! It was too dangerous. They were crazy.

Madame Rousset. We thought so and we were fearful for their safety, for we knew how vicious the Germans were those days. The jeep went down the valley very slowly since no one in the jeep knew where the Germans were that particular day. Were they in Briançon? Were they in the valley? In the streets of one of the village Robert found one member of the F.F.I., a young mechanic, who jumped in the jeep. Now they were six who soon arrived at the top of the old town. There they left the jeep and walked a few feet, then hid behind old trees. One of the Americans fired a shot to find out where the Germans were. No answer. But after the fourth shot there was an answer and the Americans jumped in their jeep, made a U-turn and went back up the valley.

Alain C. With Robert?

Madame Rousset. Yes and with the young mechanic. Well, the next day. The Americans came back with not just one jeep, but fifteen or even twenty, and with trucks. Their objective was to liberate Briançon. The battle with the German forces was very tough.

Alain C. Did the Americans lose many men?

Madame Rousset. Not really. The Germans left town, but did not go very far. They went in hiding in underground passages linking the forts above Briancon. Ignoring this, believing that the German troops had left for Italy, the Americans decided to move north and leave Briançon in the hands of the F.F.I.

Alain C. How many days did they stay?

Madame Rousset. May be eight days, may be fourteen. She asked her sister. Fernande, you were there. How long did the Americans stay in Briancon?

Fernande. I don't know. Well, I know I had enough time to make jellies. We came back from the mountains and had a lot of currants and I did make a lot of jellies.

Alain C. laughing. It must have been at least a week, right? *(In fact the American troops left Briançon after five days. They stayed from the 24th of August to the 29th.)*

Madame Rousset. The Germans came back in town. *(During the evening of the 29th)* and started to gun down people in the street. *(Among the dead were M.B.Baldenberger, the President of the Liberation Committee, and Jules Bermond, a former school mate of my brother Gilles, who attempted to protect two women using his body as a shield. He was a handsome young man and the captain of the local hockey team. What a loss! what a catastrophe!)* Many of the inhabitants of Briançon left their homes in the middle of the night in their pajamas or night gowns. Madame Bouverot, *(the wife of our athletic coach and a friend of our parents and of the Roussets),* arrived at our home in her night gown and an old coat. For a few days *(six exactly)* Briançon was a ball of fire. Facing the enraged German troops were F.F.I forces and some Americans who had not left town. The French realized that the best way to defeat the Germans was to wait a few days. The Germans were isolated, their supply route through Italy having been cut. Food and ammunition would become scarce.

At this particular time, Robert decided to get Fernande out of Briançon. She lived next to the railway station. When he got there he found to his delight that contingents of the First French Army, which had come north from the French Riviera, had arrived in town. Robert helped Fernande to reach the road to Le Monêtier where she arrived about two hours later.

The battle for liberating Briançon became intensive. Fighting was house by house. French people could see through their second floor windows where the Germans were in the streets and so they gestured to the French soldiers to go on or hide depending on the situation.

Alain C. A typical street fighting.

Madame Rousset. Exactly. Finally the German troops left town and again got inside the forts. They had to be dislodged from there. The job was given to the Touaregs *(fierce Moroccan fighters, part of the First Army)*, who were told not to take any prisoners. The Touaregs are ferocious soldiers, impressive by their size and the way they use their knives. One night, *(It was the 6th of September)*, they climbed the steep remparts of Le Fort des Tetes, barefooted holding their knives in their teeth. Though they were under intensive machine gun fire from the enemy they succeeded in taking over not only the Fort des Tetes but the other two forts. The Germans who escaped the fury of the Touaregs escaped through underground tunnels that led to the outside above the forts and this time they never came back. Many of us after the battle went to investigate these underground trenches which we did not know existed. And this is how American and French troops liberated Briançon.

Alain C. For the second time.

Madame Rousset. Right. The first time, the Americans, though they came in force, did not succeed because they failed to realize that there were underground passages around the forts which were ideal places for the Germans to hide. The second time the F.F.I. and the First Army were successful.

During the whole process of the liberation of Briançon, its inhabitants had made French and American Flags that they hoisted when the French took over the town. They took them down when the Germans were back in the streets, and hoisted them again when the town was liberated again.

Alain C. That must have been a sight all right.
During that time the rest of the Hautes Alpes was liberated and the Italian border was then defended from possible German attacks by the F.F.I. forces which soon become incorporated in the regular French Forces.

Madame Rousset continued. The French First Army left and Briançon was now in the hands of a new French administration.

Alain C. Le Monétier did not really suffer. Is that right?

Madame Rousset. Yes. Fortunately for us, our village did not experience the destruction that affected the villages down the valley, St.Chaffrey, Puy St.Pierre, Cervierres and Forville.

The sad part of the liberation was that there were a lot of town people who never were part of the Resistance, but on that day claimed to have been. They wore F.F.I.armbands, when in fact they had been collaborators or at least neutrals.

Alain C. They were the Resisters of the last hour. The same happened at Antibes. After my discharge from the Airforce in December 1945, I came back to Roquebrune-Cap Martin where my Parents had returned a year before. A few weeks later I visited Antibes and looked up a good friend of mine, Alain Cianfanelli, who had been in the underground from its early days. Barely fifteen years old then, he spied for the British. Both of us went to the cemetery of Antibes where most of our friends, who had participated in the underground were buried. It made us bitter and sad that those who had not participated in the underground were alive and bragging about their exploits.

Madame Rousset. We share your feelings. This was a phenomenon all across France. Of course, some of the collaborators, in particular those who had given the names of the Resistance fighters to the Gestapo, had been eliminated by members of the underground. An example of this concerned the daughter of a couple who had an important jewelry shop. She was always well dressed even during the war. Obviously she was not getting her dresses in France, where none were available, but in Italy, where she was often partying. We were sure that she had sold out many resistant fighters *(She had given names of young people who soon after were arrested and shot by the Italian or German police)*. Well, one morning two young men- not from Briançon-came into the jewelry shop, asked her if she was Miss Candote. She answered yes and was killed on the spot. The young men disappeared through the small streets of the Old town.

The Germans called this killing a terrorist act, but it was an act of revenge, for the underground at Briançon never really killed a German soldier in cold blood. We did not want any reprisals against the population. We did not want innocent victims. Only those who sold out members of the underground were in a few cases executed. This was the case of this young woman whose body was transported across the Italian border and buried in Italy.

Alain C. Was she a woman from here?

Madame Rousset. Oh yes! She was born here, but was of Italian ancestry. Her family had been in the jewelry business for two generations. Well, I was told that there was to be a lot of rejoicing in downtown Briançon and I wanted to be there. However, Robert advised me not to go because there were lots of personal settlements where people took the law into their own hands, a situation that reminded him of what happened during the French revolution of 1789.

Well, Alain I have to tell you another story that just came to my mind.

The teleferic of Serres Chevaliers *(a teleferic is a special ski lift)* was not finished in 1939. When the Germans occupied the region, they pressured the French to finish it, for they needed it to train their troops for the Russian front. But the French skiers, could also use it. You know that since you used it yourself. Well, Robert who was a passionate skier, as you remember, met on the slopes a lot of German skiers. Among them was a young man, who was believed to be a S.S. lieutenant. This man was very congenial and polite, always asking if Robert wanted to be the first to go down the slope. Sometimes both of them had lunch on the slopes. The lieutenant who had far more food than Robert often asked him if he wanted to share his lunch. Robert always refused.

The week of the liberation of Briançon Robert found himself down at St.Catherine, near the Railway Station. A door from a building opened and who came out but the S.S.lieutenant. Both looked at each other and decided to ignore each other and they went in different directions.

Alain C. This is not a unique example when Germans and French, for some personal reason, refused to fight each other. But there is something that needs some clarification. Did Robert have a military uniform?

Madame Rousset. No. But the S.S. lieutenant did not have any doubt that Robert was a member of the French military forces. Robert had a revolver in his hand. They simply ignored each other as the battle continued around them. Robert told me later that he did not have the heart to kill the S.S. officer because they had something in common, the love of sport. Obviously the German lieutenant must have shared the same feelings.

Alain C. What a human story!

Madame Rousset. It was an exciting time. A time for horrors and friend-ships. We shared food with perfect strangers who were helping us in many ways, delivering messages, bringing us news, alerting us to dangers, fight-ing with us. There have been true cases of devotion. It was a period of brotherly love. Unfortunately this did not last. Robert used to say: "After the war we will all love each other." Poor fellow, he had his illusions. .